FIGHT KYOTO

THE PLAN TO PROTECT
OUR ECONOMIC FUTURE

FIGHT KYOTO

THE PLAN TO PROTECT
OUR ECONOMIC FUTURE

Ezra Levant

JMCK Publishing
Calgary

FIGHT KYOTO

Copyright © 2002, Ezra Levant

First printing, November 2002
Second printing, January 2003

National Library of Canada Cataloguing in Publication

Levant, Ezra, 1972-
        Fight Kyoto : the plan to protect our economy / Ezra Levant.

Includes bibliographical references and index.
ISBN 0-9732050-0-8.—ISBN 1-55306-546-8 (LSI ed.)

        1. Greenhouse gas mitigation—Economic aspects—Canada. 2. Environmental policy—Economic aspects—Canada. 3. United Nations Framework Convention on Climate Change (1992). Protocols, etc., 1997 Dec. 11. 4. Economic forecasting--Canada. I. Title.

HC120.E5L49 2002   363.738'7456'0971   C2002-905858-9

For more information or to order copies, contact:

JMCK Publishing
Fight Kyoto Order Processing Centre
Suite 130, 919 Centre Street N.W.
Calgary, Alberta, Canada T2E 2P6
Toll free: (866) 520-5222 • Fax: (403) 520-5227
Website: www.fightkyoto.com

Printed in Canada by *Essence Publishing*

Table of Contents

Acknowledgments

There are many people I would like to thank.

My wife, Golda, was supportive when I set aside other priorities to finish the book in time to meet the urgent publishing schedule. Special thanks also to my parents, Marvin and Leslie, for their help and support.

JMCK Publishing took *Fight Kyoto* from an idea to bookshelves faster than most publishing houses would have thought possible. Special thanks to Sean McKinsley, Matthew Johnston and Stephen Johnston, and to Danielle Smith, JMCK Publishing's editor-in-chief. Thanks also to the team at Essence Group.

Gerald Chipeur, my colleague, friend and mentor at Chipeur Advocates, helped guide me through the constitutional labyrinth of energy politics, and was the book's legal editor.

Lorne Gunter, Canada's best-informed critic of Kyoto, was always willing to act as a sounding board for ideas and as a 24-hour hotline for checking facts. Ted Byfield, the patriarch of the oil patch, reminded me of the dangers of Kyoto to national unity.

Licia Corbella, Chris Nelson and Paul Jackson of the *Calgary Sun* gave me their personal support and public exposure.

Gwyn Morgan, EnCana's CEO, showed me that Kyoto endangered all Canadians, not just Albertans.

John Gardner, who designed www.fightkyoto.com, built a wave of Internet excitement that started even before the book was available in hard copy, and the principled web-mistresses at www.freedominion.ca generously host our on-line chat group. John also designed the cover, with artistic input from Kevin Libin. Thanks also to Link Byfield, Clinton Desveaux and Colby Cosh for publicizing the website. Tom Zarokostas provided technical support for our promotional effort.

Dr. Faron Ellis shared his polling insights.

Al, Jerry and Jim Korchinski and Robert Stokowski showed me how Kyoto would affect real Canadian businesses.

Special thanks to Michael Cooper, Jonathan Denis, Mike Cust, Rochelle Marshall, Ben Carter, Alim Merali, Pierre Poilievre, Jamie Tronnes, Vern and Judith Johnson, Jeremy Harrison, Gordon and Maxine Hollingshead, Dr. Robert Faltin, Glenn and Gloria Feagan, Doug Sharpe, Fritz Koenig, Sean Freeland and Dave Freeland for their personal support.

Mark Buzan helped collect historical information about the National Energy Program.

Literally hundreds of people from across Canada sent me information about Kyoto, ranging from in-depth scientific analysis, to anecdotes about how the treaty would affect them. Others simply wanted to wish me well, and let me know they wanted to join the fight. I would like to thank them here.

Raymond J. Addington, O.B.E.—Aldergrove, British Columbia

Tom Harris—Ottawa, Ontario

Dr. Adrian Wade—Richmond, British Columbia

Charles Schafer, PhD—Waverley, Nova Scotia

Dr. Ian Boothe—Edmonton, Alberta

Ross Harriman—Airdrie, Alberta

Gary Del Villano—Carleton Place, Ontario

Lanny Westersund—Calgary, Alberta

Bill Whitney—Fort McMurray, Alberta

Kevin Miller—Calgary, Alberta

Pavel Michenka—Calgary, Alberta

Bruce Audley—Sherwood Park, Alberta

David A. MacKay—Beaverlodge, Alberta

Freda & Stewart Ewen—Black Diamond, Alberta

Michael J. Collins—St. John's, Newfoundland

Brian Posehn—Calgary, Alberta

Rita Tassé—Hull, Quebec

Norman & Terry Tropak—Vegreville, Alberta

Paul Berg—Yorkton, Saskatchewan

Rudolph R. Stea, PhD—Halifax, Nova Scotia

Chris J. Ott—Calgary, Alberta

Ted & Rose d'Haêne—Airdrie, Alberta

Don L. Scott—Calgary, Alberta

Lorne Samson—Calgary, Alberta

Cornelis B. de Leeuw—Calgary, Alberta

Richard Van Seters—Markham, Ontario

Brian Gropp—Stratford, Ontario

Paul Hunter—Winnipeg, Manitoba

Robert Dodds—Mississauga, Ontario
Mark Parsons—Edmonton, Alberta
Alexei Jernov—Edmonton, Alberta
Jane Goddard—Calgary, Alberta
Connie Wilkins—Kingston, Ontario
Mike Maguire—Kars, Ontario
Bruce Kerr—Sherwood Park, Alberta
William McBeath—Edmonton, Alberta
Kathy & Maurice Fitzgerald—Edmonton, Alberta
Siobhain Broekhoven-Fiene—Howe Island, Ontario
Éric Duhaime—St-Eustache, Quebec
Andrew Banks—Greenwood, Nova Scotia
John Boettger—Toronto, Ontario
Bonnie Johnston—Edmonton, Alberta
William Burk—Saint John, New Brunswick
Ryan Lamarche—Red Deer, Alberta
Kasra Nejatian—Kingston, Ontario
Bob Wood—St. Albert, Alberta
Patricia Burgess—St. Albert, Alberta
Don Marcotte—Edmonton, Alberta
Dr. Roy L. Rasmussen—Calgary, Alberta
William Robson—Toronto, Ontario
Peter D. Schalin—Edmonton, Alberta
Alan Cranfield—Toronto, Ontario
Jack Morrow—Edmonton, Alberta
Ken Conrad—Mill Bay, British Columbia
Jason Kauppinen—Kingston, Ontario
Garry Galinsky—Calgary, Alberta
Doug & Sally Sharpe—Calgary, Alberta

Joel Loh—Calgary, Alberta
Dennis Young—Grande Prairie, Alberta
David McCallum—Edmonton, Alberta
Rachael Van Kesteren—Chatham, Ontario
Walter Robinson—Ottawa, Ontario
Jerry Votypka—Calgary, Alberta
Jane Lidster—Calgary, Alberta
Conrad J. Zarowny—Calgary, Alberta
Olav Cramer—Calgary, Alberta
Simon Chapelle—Newmarket, Ontario
Todd Krohman—Langley, British Columbia
Wes Andrews—Calgary, Alberta
Robert Hamby—Calgary, Alberta
Glenn Woiceshyn—Calgary, Alberta
Jeff Dick—Edmonton, Alberta
Mark Wickens—Toronto, Ontario
Ken Cheveldayoff—Saskatoon, Saskatchewan
Brian Parker—Calgary, Alberta
Michael J. Belich—Calgary, Alberta
Gail Parker—Calgary, Alberta
Shane McAllister—Calgary, Alberta
David Ryan—Calgary, Alberta
Philip Beaudoin—Toronto, Ontario
Tim Calon—Drumheller, Alberta
John Beishlag—Toronto, Ontario
Michael P. Ivy—Edmonton, Alberta
Robin Wilcox—Edmonton, Alberta
Sid Parkinson—Montreal, Quebec
Kathleen Lust—Calgary, Alberta

Mark Gray—Calgary, Alberta
Ben Klippenstein—Edmonton, Alberta
Charles Davies—Calgary, Alberta
Dr. Matthew Dunchuk—Edmonton, Alberta
Patricia Langmuir Taylor—Toronto, Ontario
Ian E. Bush—Ottawa, Ontario
Bob McCrossan—Mill Bay, British Columbia
W. Robert Dengler—Aurora, Ontario
Doug Hafso—Edmonton, Alberta
David Usherwood—Cochrane, Alberta
Roy Beyer—Edmonton, Alberta
Gary Schalin—Edmonton, Alberta
David Klassen—Flatbush, Alberta
Carlos and Patricia del Carpio—Calgary, Alberta
Raymond E. Killeen—Edmonton, Alberta
Troy Lanigan—Regina, Saskatchewan
Doug and Sharon Smith—Calgary, Alberta
Dr. Vikas Mehrotra—Edmonton, Alberta

Prologue

LIBERALS REVOLT AS KYOTO DEADLINE LOOMS
"Canada must obey, or face sanctions," says
UN Secretary-General Jean Chrétien

The National Globe,
January 25, 2012, page A1.

OTTAWA—Prime Minister Paul Martin could face a full-blown rebellion at today's caucus meeting, warn dissident Liberal MPs who are upset over the government's iron-fisted approach to implementing the United Nations Kyoto Protocol.

"When General Motors announced it was phasing out its Canadian production and building its new SUV line in the U.S., you'd think Martin would have got the message," said one Ontario Liberal MP, who spoke on condition of anonymity. "We're still only half way to our Kyoto targets, but unemployment has already touched 10 per cent. If Martin won't stop himself, we will," added the MP, who said "more than thirty" other Liberals plan to challenge the Prime Minister at this morning's party caucus meeting.

The Kyoto Protocol, a treaty signed in 1997 by Mr. Martin's predecessor, Jean Chrétien, requires Canada to

13

drastically reduce its emissions of gases such as carbon dioxide, which is generated from cars and factories, as well as from animals and even human breathing.

This year marks the treaty's deadline for Canada to cut emissions by 30 per cent, but Mr. Martin's program—called draconian by business and agricultural leaders, as well as taxpayer advocates—has reduced emissions by only 14 per cent. Government documents obtained by the National Globe through access to information show that much of that reduction has been unintentionally achieved through a series of industrial bankruptcies, which forced the closure in 2008 of the Dofasco and Stelco plants in Hamilton, Ontario and Contrecoeur, Quebec and the loss of 400 dairy and hog farms across the country since 2009.

Complicating matters for Mr. Martin is the fact that Mr. Chrétien is now the United Nations Secretary-General, which makes him the global diplomat in charge of enforcing the treaty.

"Canadian politicians must obey international law, or face sanctions," said Mr. Chrétien, reached by the National Globe yesterday at his New York apartment. "Kyoto was a commitment Canada made in 2002, and a promise is a promise. Just because I am Canadian doesn't mean I will let Canada or my old friend Paul off the hook."

Mr. Chrétien pointed out that Mr. Martin himself attended the United Nations Earth Summit twenty years ago, when the global plan to reduce greenhouse gas reductions was first drafted by Maurice Strong, a Canadian businessman-diplomat and Mr. Martin's family friend and mentor. "Maurice gave Paul his start in life—his money and connections," said Mr. Chrétien. "Now it's time for Paul to give something back. That means implementing Kyoto."

One MP who has been an increasingly vocal critic of Mr. Martin's Kyoto plan is David Kilgour, the independent MP from Edmonton Southeast. Mr. Kilgour was ousted from the Liberal cabinet and had his party membership revoked after he voted against the government's 2006 budget, because it contained a 50-cent-per-litre environment tax on gasoline.

"Kyoto has caused a national recession that has left no province untouched," said Mr. Kilgour. "But as an Albertan, I just can't support a Liberal policy that has destroyed the energy industry for the second time in a generation," he said, referring to the National Energy Program of the 1980s. Mr. Kilgour joined the Liberal party after he was expelled from the Progressive Conservative party in 1991 for voting against the GST.

Adding momentum to the caucus revolt is a grassroots campaign launched last week by the Ottawa-based International Taxpayers Federation. "Kyoto has raised taxes for the average Canadian family by $4,400 per year," said Walter Robinson, the ITF's president. "Between taxes on parking stalls, taxes on SUVs and pickup trucks, taxes on gasoline, heating oil and natural gas, and the new toll booths on the Trans-Canada Highway, Canadian families are poorer, and Canadian businesses are leaving for the U.S."

"Kyoto regulations have made matters even worse," added Robinson. "Between forced carpooling and the new 'sweater regulation' that requires homes to be kept to a brisk 15 degrees Celsius in the winter, we Canadians have lost many of our freedoms."

Robinson's campaign and the divisions in the Liberal caucus have been seized upon by the opposition Alliance-

Conservative coalition. "Kyoto isn't just bad economic policy," said AC co-leader Stephen Harper. "It's also bad environmental policy. Even if we meet our Kyoto targets, most of the world's economies are exempt—including the U.S., China, India and Brazil. In ten days, their unchecked gas emissions undo any reductions we've made here in Canada over a decade at great cost."

Peter MacKay, the AC's other co-leader, claimed that Mr. Martin's Kyoto plan had killed Atlantic Canada's best chance for economic self-sufficiency. "Just when Nova Scotia and Newfoundland were starting to see private sector investment in our off-shore oil rigs—and the jobs that come with them—Kyoto taxes and regulations put all the projects on hold. When Inco shut in the Voisey's Bay project because it couldn't meet emissions standards, 2,000 men were laid off in a month. No wonder the Newfoundland Independence Party is polling at 34 per cent—higher than the Western Separatist Party was when they became Alberta's Official Opposition back in 2008."

Mr. Martin would not comment to the media, but his Environment Minister, Louise Comeau, told the National Globe that while she sympathized with Liberal backbenchers' concerns, the matter was no longer within Parliament's control. "When we signed the Kyoto treaty in December 1997, and ratified it five years later, it became Canadian law. And, under the terms of the United Nations Enforcement Protocol of 2007, any politician that does not implement the treaty can be brought before the International Criminal Court, and charged with Eco-Crimes. I'm certainly not going to be the first Canadian hauled before the ICC—and I don't think our nervous nellies on the back-bench want to be, either."

The Prime Minister has scheduled a press conference on the matter for today after his morning caucus meeting.

* * * * *

Come on—a new 50-cent-per-litre gas tax? Get real.

Steel mills and auto factories being shut down in the midst of a recession? Taxes on SUVs? Government orders to turn down the thermostat? A new parking lot tax? Surely this unhappy future can't be Canada's destiny. The Kyoto Protocol won't do that.

Or will it?

Jean Chrétien, the Prime Minister, has vowed to ratify the Kyoto Protocol in the House of Commons as soon as possible. That would make the treaty Canadian law—and legally oblige Canadians to cut back on our emissions of carbon dioxide and other "greenhouse gases" by 30 per cent over the next ten years.

Thirty per cent may not sound like a lot, but when you look at all of the activities that emit these Kyoto gases, the audacity of the plan becomes apparent: Everything from heating your home, to driving your car, to breathing generates carbon dioxide—and the sum of those emissions has to be cut back by 30 per cent, or 240 million tonnes of carbon dioxide. Since breathing 30 per cent less is out, other drastic measures are necessary to meet the law of Kyoto.

The United Nations Enforcement Protocol of 2007 is not reality, and Jean Chrétien is not the Secretary-General of the United Nations—at least not yet. But every other economic and environmental fact in that news story from the future is based on an actual Government of Canada Kyoto study or proposal.

Implementing Kyoto will cause a recession. That's not fear-mongering from Canadian businesses. That is the conclusion of a team of federal economists hired by federal Environment Minister David Anderson, Canada's most fanatical pro-Kyoto activist.

That same government study said that one of the only ways to get Canadians to cut back on driving so much is to jack up gasoline prices to $1.10 per litre. Again, that's not propaganda from conservative politicians. That's straight from the government's own Kyoto studies.

Kyoto will be the first foreign treaty Canada's Parliament has ever ratified before the fine print is even written: ready, fire, aim.

SUV taxes? A trial balloon floated in the press by the government in September 2002. Steel mills closing? That's from another government study, published in November 2000 that predicted Kyoto would kill 30,000 steel jobs in Ontario alone.

Farms shut down? Given that Kyoto regulates carbon dioxide and methane—two gases that animals naturally emit—it's not surprising to learn that Canadian livestock is responsible for the emission of gases equalling one-twelfth of Canada's required cutbacks.

A $2 per day parking tax on all parking stalls in the country? It's one way to get people to stop driving, and it's being debated by Ottawa as a solution. So is asking Canadians to turn down the heat at home; so is having police enforce carpooling on major roadways; so are a dozen other heavy-handed laws. Each of these is detailed in later chapters.

No one knows what the final Kyoto laws, taxes and regulations will be—not even Chrétien himself. They haven't been determined yet, but that hasn't stopped the government from blazing ahead with the law. "The ratification issue is separate from the development of a plan,"[1] admitted David Anderson, the Environment Minister. That's a 180-degree turn from Anderson's promise on national television in March 2002, when Peter Mansbridge asked him if he'd have the details of the plan—including the costs—worked out. "Absolutely, Peter,"[2] he answered, "before there is any ratification." It wasn't the truth, but at least it got the Minister through the interview without losing face.

Kyoto will be the first foreign treaty Canada's Parliament has ever ratified before the fine print is even written: ready, fire, aim. Or, as Alberta Premier Ralph Klein, an opponent of Kyoto, said, "It's like signing a mortgage for a property you have never seen and for a price that you have never discussed."[3]

The Canada-U.S. Free Trade Agreement—the only other treaty with a comparable economic impact—was pored over line by line in Parliament before being ratified, and was the main subject of the entire 1988 federal election. Every Canadian knew what free trade meant, whether they agreed with it or not. When it comes to Kyoto, a majority of Canadians tell pollsters they still haven't even heard of it.

Kyoto will cause a recession. It will restrict every Canadian's daily life. The implementation plan hasn't even been written. But here it comes.

---

[1] David Anderson, press conference at the Halifax Environment and Natural Resources Ministers meeting, October 29, 2002.

[2] David Anderson, *The National*, CBC, March 12, 2002.

[3] "Why Alberta opposes the Kyoto Protocol," Government of Alberta, 2002.

Before the end of this year, the government will bring forward a resolution to Parliament on the issue of ratifying the Kyoto Protocol on Climate Change. Meeting this challenge must become a national project, calling upon the efforts and contributions of all Canadians, in all regions and sectors of the economy—producers and consumers, governments and citizens.[4]

So said the government's Throne Speech, delivered to mark the start of Parliament at the end of September 2002. Kyoto forces Canadians to cut back on our energy use. But the royal warning was clear: This isn't just targeting "big business" or the energy industry. Everyone's going to pay a price for Kyoto.

Still don't believe $1.10 gasoline, mandatory carpooling and taxes, taxes, taxes are the future of a Kyoto Canada? Here's what Chrétien had to say in his Parliamentary reply to the Throne Speech: "Citizens and consumers are ready to adjust their behaviour. Mr. Speaker, it will not be easy."[5]

Adjust our behaviour? Can there be any clearer warning than that? Coming from Jean Chrétien—a lame-duck Prime Minister, looking for a legacy and not too concerned about leaving a political and economic mess for his successor—a demand that Canadians "adjust" our behaviour is worrisome.

How much of an adjustment will be necessary? "We will have a strategy in place that allows us to meet our obligations by 2012," he said. That means a 30 per cent adjustment.

---

4 Governor-General, *Speech from the Throne*, Ottawa, September 30, 2002.

5 Jean Chrétien, *Hansard*, October 1, 2002.

But here's the irony: Even if Canadians "adjust" our behaviour enough to meet Kyoto's targets, the world's greenhouse emissions will continue to grow. That's because Canada is only responsible for two per cent of the world's man-made emissions—so cutting our economy by 30 per cent will only reduce 0.6 per cent of the world's emissions. The United States, China, India, Brazil, Mexico, Venezuela, Australia, Germany, Saudi Arabia and other OPEC countries, and even Japan—home of the city of Kyoto, where the treaty was signed— have either refused to sign the treaty, refuse to implement the treaty, or are exempted by the treaty from making any reductions under it.

Would Canadians have allowed our government to sign such a treaty had they known how biased it was against Canada?

Would Canadians have allowed our government to sign such a treaty, had they known how biased it was against Canada? Canadians never had the chance to make that informed decision. On December 9, 1997, Chrétien told Parliament "if there is a cost...it will be exactly the same cost to every nation signing on the dotted line."[6] Like Chrétien's promise to "scrap" the GST, it was made in the heat of the moment, to extricate the Prime Minister from a tough spot—in this case, from a difficult query in Question Period. Five years later, we now know it wasn't true. But the treaty was signed—and now it's being ratified.

That is the absurd position Canada is now in— hurtling towards ratification of an environmentally pointless law that will devastate Canada's economy.

---

6 Jean Chrétien, *Hansard*, December 9, 1997.

Fight Kyoto asks—and tries to answer—the questions that Chrétien's own MPs should be asking, but so far haven't had the courage to ask, at least in public. Here are ten big ones:

1. How did Canada come to sign such a dangerous treaty in the first place?

2. Who actually wrote the treaty—and what was their political agenda?

3. What exactly does the text of the treaty say—and how is Canada likely to implement it?

4. What is the environmental and scientific basis for the treaty? Is it sound?

5. Have Canada's media been impartial in the Kyoto debates?

6. Who are the lobbyists pushing for Kyoto?

7. What will be the economic damage to Canada if we implement Kyoto?

8. How might Kyoto actually make the world's environment dirtier?

9. Will Paul Martin implement Kyoto if he becomes Prime Minister?

And, perhaps the most important question of all:

10. Should Canadians fight Kyoto?

CHAPTER ONE

Blame It on Rio

Ten years ago, an eccentric Canadian diplomat named Maurice Strong chaired the United Nations "Earth Summit" in Rio de Janeiro, Brazil. The meeting attracted more than 100 world leaders, including Brian Mulroney, Canada's Prime Minister of the day and Paul Martin, who was then the Liberal Party's Environment critic.

As Gerald Caplan, a prominent New Democrat, said at the time, the Rio Summit

> will be, literally, the largest, most complex, international gathering of all time. Years of work have gone into preparations. Twenty-four million pages of documents have been churned out.[7]

The goal? Caplan knew it was as much about wealth redistribution as it was about environmentalism. He wrote:

> Maurice Strong, organizer of the Earth Summit, calculates that poor nations need $125 billion from 'the North' to handle their environmental problems.

---

[7] Gerald Caplan, "So much work, so little gain for Earth Summit," *The Toronto Star*, May 31, 1992, p. B3.

Elaine Dewar, a Canadian journalist who was given unprecedented access to Maurice Strong, wrote:

> I knew that over at Strong's office his staff thought $125-billion a year would be the right amount to transfer to the poor nations in the cause of sustainable development, a huge sum of money.[8]

Like so many other UN conventions, Rio turned out to be little more than an opportunity for the world's leaders to throw a big party in an exotic locale, and issue some motherhood and apple pie press releases. It was the swan song for many world leaders—including Canada's Brian Mulroney, who would retire the next year. At Rio, world leaders were told that human economic activities might be causing the world to warm up; each country's diplomats dutifully agreed to the "ultimate objective" of "stabilization of greenhouse gas concentrations in the atmosphere."[9] Al Gore, campaigning to become the U.S. Vice President, summed up the enviromania in the political air as well, in his political manifesto.[10] He wrote:

Rio turned out to be little more than an opportunity for the world's leaders to throw a big party in an exotic locale, and issue some motherhood and apple pie press releases.

---

8 Elaine Dewar, *Cloak of Green,* James Lorimer & Company Ltd., 1995, p. 298.

9 *Framework Convention on Climate Change*, United Nations, 1992.

10 Al Gore, *Earth in the Balance*, Houghton Mifflin Co., 1992, p. 275.

The struggle to save the global environment is in one way much more difficult than the struggle to vanquish Hitler, for this time the war is with ourselves. We are the enemy, just as we have only ourselves as allies.

The Rio treaty, however, contained a fudge-factor: It specifically permitted countries "to enable economic development to proceed in a sustainable manner." In short, like many UN documents, it was a hodgepodge of conflicting ideas. And in the case of Rio, it wasn't binding. The politicians came, they saw, and they sent out a press release. And then they went home and focused their attention instead on the world's recession.

That's what the politicians did; but they come and go—it is the diplomats and the bureaucrats who endure. Five years later, George H.W. Bush was gone, and so were Brian Mulroney and many other world leaders who had attended Rio. But the UN envirocrats had been meeting regularly, establishing a sort of fraternity, which hopped from world capital to world capital every year. It is the ultimate diplomatic posting. At the Johannesburg convention in 2002, for example, the 70-person U.K. delegation had a £500,000 budget, and dined at the five-star Michelangelo Hotel. "Money is no object," exulted head chef Desmond Morgan, to the delight of the British tabloids. Morgan's menu included "5,000 oysters," more than "1,000 pounds of lobster and other shellfish" and "buckets of caviar and piles of pâté de foie gras,"[11] screamed *The Sun* of London. Sixty thousand summiteers from 182 countries descended on Johannesburg, all in the name of saving the planet. Nice work, if you can find it.

---

11 Neil Syson, "Lobsters, caviar and brandy for MPs at summit on starvation," *The Sun* (London), August 27, 2002.

In 1997, the city of choice was Kyoto, and it was there that an update to the toothless Rio convention was hatched, called the Kyoto Protocol. Hatched is a more accurate word than "negotiated" in this case, because Canada's delegation of politicians, bureaucrats and environmental lobbyists went to Kyoto stating that no matter what the deal said, Canada would sign it.

That's hardly a way to enter into any agreement, let alone a massive economic and environmental treaty. But that's what Canada did.

CHAPTER TWO

Maurice Strong

The Kyoto Protocol was the work of thousands of bureaucrats, diplomats and politicians. But no one person was more responsible for it than a Canadian named Maurice Strong. Strong organized the United Nations' first world environmental summit in Stockholm, Sweden in 1972, and has never stopped pressing for a world where the UN's resolutions would be enforced as the law in every corner of the Earth. Strong went on to chair the 1992 Rio conference on global warming and to become the Senior Advisor to Kofi Annan, the UN's Secretary-General. Not bad for a kid from Oak Lake, Manitoba, who dropped out of school at age fourteen.[12]

But Strong is different than other social butterflies who flit from one UN conference to the next. He is a powerful businessman, who has served as president of such massive energy companies as Petro-Canada and Ontario Hydro, and on the board of industrial giant Toyota.[13] He is a huge political donor, not just here in Canada, but to both the

---

[12] Maurice Strong, *Where on Earth are We Going?*, Knopf Canada, 2000, p. 54.

[13] Strong, p. 397.

Republican and Democratic parties in the United States as well.[14] At age 29, he became president of Power Corporation of Canada, fusing his destiny to Canada's wealthiest and most influential families—including Paul Martin Sr. and Jr., now Canada's heir apparent to the Prime Minister. Strong hired Paul Jr. to work for him during a vacation from university.[15] "We controlled many companies, controlled political budgets," Strong said of his time at Power Corporation. "We influenced a lot of appointments. Politicians got to know you and you them."[16]

Paul Martin, Jr. has certainly kept in touch with Strong from his college days. After finishing his studies, Martin was hired as Strong's personal assistant. "I brought him into the company," said Strong, describing how he steered Martin through "a few bumpy episodes" and into "a star performer." Martin climbed the corporate ladder at Strong's company, and eventually acquired control of Canada Steamship Lines, the source of Martin's great wealth to this day. "This set the stage for his inevitable entry into political life," wrote Strong.[17]

Strong gave Martin a summer job during university; then he hired Martin into Power Corporation's executive suite. He helped guide Martin towards unimaginable personal wealth—and even predicted Martin's path to becoming Prime Minister.

But Strong's influence reaches farther than just Canada; indeed, compared to his American and European friends,

---

[14] Ronald Bailey, "International Man of Mystery," *National Review*, September 1, 1997.

[15] Strong, p. 90.

[16] Dewar, p. 270.

[17] Strong, p. 98.

Paul Martin is a junior star in Strong's constellation. Strong sits on boards with the Rockefellers and Mikhail Gorbachev; he chairs private meetings of CEOs, including Bill Gates. He hobnobs with the world's royalty, too—and with dictators and despots. He once did a business deal with arms dealer Adnan Khashoggi, and wound up with a 200,000-acre ranch in Colorado—which his wife, Hanne, runs as a New Age spiritual colony.[18] He told *Maclean's* magazine in 1976 that he was "a socialist in ideology, a capitalist in methodology." He warns that if we don't heed his environmentalist warnings, the Earth will collapse into chaos. "Do we really want this? Do we want Marx to be proven right, after all?"[19] he asks. He shares the views of the most radical environmentalist street protester, but instead of shouting himself hoarse at a police barricade outside a global conference, he's the Secretary-General inside, wielding the gavel.

> **Instead of shouting himself hoarse at a police barricade outside a global conference, he's the Secretary-General inside, wielding the gavel.**

SEIZING POWER

Strong has always courted and wielded power—but not through any shabby election campaign. He was once a Liberal candidate in the 1979 federal election, but he pulled out of the race with just a month to go before the vote. How could a mere Canadian Member of Parliament wield the kind of international control that he had tasted in Stockholm?

---

[18] Bailey, 1997.

[19] Strong, p. 26.

Journalist Elaine Dewar, who interviewed Strong at length about his ambitions, described why Strong loved the UN so much. "He could raise his own money from whomever he liked, appoint anyone he wanted, control the agenda," wrote Dewar of her interview.

He told me he had more unfettered power than a cabinet minister in Ottawa. He was right: no voters had put him in office, he didn't have to run for re-election, yet he could profoundly affect many lives.[20]

Strong prefers power that is extracted from democracies, and kept safely away from unenlightened voters. In his recent autobiography, Strong complained that his would-be constituents just didn't get it.

I shouldn't have been surprised that the constituents of suburban Scarborough didn't have the same interests or priorities that I did...my constituents' priorities were parochial, their focus being the direct impact of government policies on them...

My speeches on the environment went over like so many lead balloons. They wanted to hear my views on the very local and the very here-and-now.[21]

There is a common thread that runs through the dozens of organizations he leads or supports: none of them are merely national in nature, and all of them believe in "global governance." That is the diplomatic way of describing decision-making by self-selected world leaders, as opposed to democratically elected national or local

[20] Dewar, p. 278.

[21] Strong, p. 152.

leaders. "A new paradigm of cooperative global governance is the only feasible basis" for running the earth, Strong announced recently at an "Earth Dialogues Forum" in France.[22] His Earth Charter would replace national constitutions as the supreme law of the planet. International treaties, such as Kyoto, would be enforced around the world with just as much authority as local laws, like a country's Income Tax Act or Criminal Code. Of course, there would be global taxes, too, to pay for it all—with taxes on financial transactions or energy being the most commonly suggested.[23] "We recommend that there will be a kind of tax...in dealing with climate change," Strong told journalist Dewar.[24]

To camouflage the UN's taxation without democratic representation, Strong had pumped millions of dollars into so-called Non-Governmental Organizations, or NGOs. The money often came directly from the UN, or from the many organizations or foundations in which Strong was a member or director. Ironically, many Non-Governmental Organizations were actually funded by governments—a truly Orwellian hypocrisy.

Most power-crazed men would stop at calling for a one-world Earth Charter to replace the U.S. Constitution, or the UN Charter. But in an interview with his own Earth Charter Commission, Strong said:

> The real goal of the Earth Charter is that it will in fact become like the Ten Commandments...It will become a

---

[22] "Notes for the Plenary Address by Maurice F. Strong," *Earth Dialogues Forum*, Lyon, France, February 21, 2002.

[23] Bailey, 1997.

[24] Dewar, p. 294.

symbol of the aspirations and the commitments of people everywhere.[25]

Sounds like Maurice has been hanging out at his Colorado spirit ranch without his sun hat on.

There has been no one like Maurice Strong before, except perhaps in fiction—Ernst Blofeld comes to mind, 007's round-faced nemesis in *You Only Live Twice* and other James Bond movies. But Blofeld always sought to attack the world order, to challenge it from some remote hideaway—not to co-opt it, and transform it from the inside as Strong does. Blofeld would threaten a meeting of the United Nations; Strong would chair that meeting and carefully script its agenda. Strong is by far the smarter of the two.

Strangely, Strong once indulged his inner Blofeld, musing to a stunned reporter about a violent plot to take over the world through one of his many super-organizations. In 1990, he told a reporter a fantasy scenario for the World Economic Forum meeting in Davos, Switzerland—where 1,000 diplomats, CEOs and politicians gather "to address global issues." Strong, naturally, is on the board of the World Economic Forum; it is one of those capitalist tools that he hopes to harness for his socialist aims.[26]

> What if a small group of these world leaders were to conclude that the principal risk to the earth comes from the actions of the rich countries?...

---

[25] Maurice Strong, "People's Earth Charter," March 5, 1998. On-line posting. *The Earth Charter Initiative.* <http://www.earthcharter.org>

[26] On-line posting. *World Economic Forum.* <http://www.weforum.org>

In order to save the planet, the group decides: Isn't the only hope for the planet that the industrialized civilizations collapse? Isn't it our responsibility to bring this about?[27]

That's Strong talking, but those are Blofeld's words coming out. It sounds like a SPECTRE plan. But this is no fictitious Bond movie villain speaking—it is the real man who chaired the Rio Earth Summit and who is Kofi Annan's senior advisor.

> **Strong once said… "Isn't the only hope for the planet that the industrialized civilizations collapse?"**

"This group of world leaders forms a secret society to bring about an economic collapse," continued Strong, warming to his fantasy.

It's February. They're all at Davos. These aren't terrorists. They're world leaders. They have positioned themselves in the world's commodities and stock markets. They've engineered, using their access to stock markets and computers and gold supplies, a panic. Then, they prevent the world's stock markets from closing. They jam the gears. They hire mercenaries who hold the rest of the world leaders at Davos as hostage. The markets can't close…

Strong catches himself. "I probably shouldn't be saying things like this." But is fantasizing about holding the world hostage, like Dr. Evil in an Austin Powers movie, any less strange than Maurice Strong's other solutions to environmental problems?

---

[27] Daniel Wood, "The Wizard of the Baca Grande," *West Magazine* May 1990.

DO AS I SAY, DON'T DO AS I DO

In 1972, when Strong was organizing the first environmental conference for the UN in Stockholm, he granted an interview to London's BBC. "I am convinced that the prophets of doom have to be taken seriously,"[28] he said. The only way to avoid doomsday, said Strong, was if

> man, in light of this evidence, is going to be wise enough and enlightened enough to subject himself to this kind of discipline and control.

That discipline and control, of course, would be meted out by supernational organizations such as the UN.

Just like his interview at Davos, Strong warmed to his topic. The BBC reporter asked him what kind of discipline and control people could expect—would it include legal limits on the number of children that a family could have? Strong explained:

> Licenses to have babies incidentally is something that I got in trouble for some years ago for suggesting even in Canada that this might be necessary at some point, at least some restriction on the right to have a child.

But, if the world didn't follow his instructions—if governments didn't heed the warnings of the doomsayers—then "this is one of the possible courses that society would have to seriously consider." Strong himself has five children.

Nearly thirty years later, Strong was still clinging to his depressing vision of the future—even though his nightmare predictions from a generation earlier had failed to materi-

---

28 On-line posting. BBC News.
<http://news.bbc.co.uk/1/hi/sci/tec/2164240.stm>

alize. In his semi-autobiographical book, *Where on Earth Are We Going*, Strong writes a "report" dated January 1, 2031. Mankind had caused extreme climate change that "caused more damage than both world wars of the twentieth century," he wrote. "Water vendors" need armed guards to keep back Americans dying of thirst. Malaria and heat waves kill off Americans by the hundreds of thousands—and two thirds of all humans perish. Strong didn't need the baby licenses after all—Mother Nature took care of that. Incredibly, Strong says this culling of the human herd is a "glimmer of hope for the future of our species and its potential for regeneration." (Kofi Annan, the UN Secretary-General, wrote the foreword to this Jim Jones-style screed.) And, coincidentally, the renewal in Strong's book finds its genesis in Crestone, Colorado, at the 200,000-acre "spiritual retreat" run by Strong's wife—the American "haven for the virtues of sustainability, harmony and 'ethical husbandry.'"[29] After all, he writes, "we are all gods now, gods in charge of our own destiny."[30] That must be some spiritual retreat.

That Strong's fantasy future includes his own ranch in a starring role is no surprise; he has always blended his private interests with public causes, using his government and UN connections to set up for-profit environmental companies. His conflicts of interest would be enough for a cabinet minister to resign from elected office. But, of course, nobody elected Strong.

Exploiting the industrial and commercial value of the water aquifers beneath his Colorado spirit ranch isn't a con-

---

[29] Strong, p. 19.

[30] Strong, p. 29.

flict of interest, of course. But it is an example of a hypocritical do-as-I-say, don't-do-as-I-do policy. Just like Strong demands that ordinary people reduce their consumption of resources, while he leads a jet-setting lifestyle, his call for the conservation of resources stops at his own farm.

Strong demands that ordinary people reduce their consumption of resources, while he leads a jet-setting lifestyle, his call for the conservation of resources stops at his own farm.

Strong—who warns that water will be rationed by armed guards by 2031—was eager to exploit "the immense groundwater reservoir that underlies" his ranch, and he put together a group of high-flying investors, and formed a company called American Water Development. All of a sudden the man who believes that capitalism and property rights lead to environmental degradation concluded that:

> If we wanted to protect our water rights, we would have to develop them or they could be claimed by others.[31]

Strong's corporation got into a scuffle with local environmentalists, the U.S. government, and "immediately drew the hostility and active opposition of most of the people in the valley." He pulled out of the project, and his share netted $2.5-million, which Strong had shuffled to an eco-spiritual foundation. After that, American Water Development lost its court battle to exploit the water, and was abandoned, having lost close to $20-million. Strong believes in communal rationing of resources, economic min-

---

[31] Strong, pp. 161-165.

imalism, and global governance trumping local rights. But when it came to his company, his water, and his financial plans, he had no compunction about fighting against his neighbours, local environmentalists, the U.S. government and eventually, his own partners in the deal.

When his old friend Bob Rae, then the Premier of Ontario, hired Strong to run the massive Hydro Ontario utility, Strong did so on the condition that he could continue to run his own corporate affairs, and gallivant around the globe. That type of arrangement was ideal for Strong—it gave him a handsome personal income, an official position of authority, and a great opportunity to network. But the deal he struck with Rae also relieved him of onerous responsibilities to the voters and taxpayers—just Strong's style. As Tom Walkom wrote in his definitive history of the Rae government:

> At the height of the 1993 social contract talks, for instance, the government's chief negotiator, Michael Decter, needed urgently to talk to the Hydro chairman. Strong was nowhere to be found; he was, Decter was told, incommunicado somewhere in Europe. In frustration, Decter finally turned to Rae. Did the premier have any advice on how to get a hold of the Hydro chairman? Rae's rye response was not that helpful... "My advice Mike," he told Decter, "is to go to the nearest hub airport and wait. He'll probably be through.[32]

Strong knows how he is viewed by opponents to his radical environmentalism, or his promotion of a UN government with taxation and enforcement powers that trump national governments. And he seems to rather enjoy being

---

[32] Thomas Walkom, *Rae Days*, Key Porter Books, 1994, p. 255.

described as a man at the center of international intrigue and secretive power-brokering, away from the prying eyes of voters. Says the self-conscious Strong:

> Sure, these are but the deluded and paranoid ravings of the Western far right, and I wouldn't normally trouble to mention them at all…

> Except that my reaction when I hear a few of these charges is that I wish I had a smidgen of the power (and money!) they say I have. I wish I could accomplish a few of the things they already attribute to me…I do wish I could assist my many friends and colleagues in all the organizations I belong to, to remake the political and economic landscape.[33]

But this is Strong feigning modesty, and not very convincingly. But this is Strong feigning modesty, and not very convincingly. Later in his autobiography he reprints his ostentatious seven-page resume, boasting every connection he has. His book takes name-dropping to a new level, including a seven-page "name index," a list of literally hundreds of blue-chip associates that Strong has in his Rolodex.

From time to time in his book, Strong realizes that his personal belief that "we are all gods now" might strike the average reader as somewhat pompous. That's when he protests that he doesn't have all the power that his foes ascribe to him—and that, for example, he even enjoys taking public transit when he has a chance, and that his crusade to save the world involves some asceticism, not just

---

[33] Strong, p. 46.

first-class airfare and five-star hotels. A few pages later, of course, the proletarian pretense is dropped, and he just can't resist recounting how he once racked up a massive limousine bill, and passed it off to Ontario taxpayers.

> I appreciate that $700 seems a lot for a limousine service—conjuring up fat-cat-images of sleek black limos with uniformed chauffeurs—but this one was very modest...I've always made a habit of living modestly, even when traveling on expense accounts.[34]

In most social settings, a compulsive name-dropper or braggart turns people off; at the United Nations, of course, it is a coveted personality trait and a sign of great potential for upward mobility. And nobody does it better than Strong.

Maurice Strong: a Dr. Evil-style strategist for the industrial collapse of the world from high in the Swiss Alps. Owner of a 200,000 acre New Age zen colony. Designer of a proposal to "seriously consider" requiring licenses to have babies. This is the architect of the Kyoto Protocol.

---

[34] Strong, pp. 274-275.

CHAPTER THREE

The U.S. Senate Decides to Fight

Five months before the Kyoto conference, the U.S. Senate did something that Canada's House of Commons (or Senate, for that matter) did not do. They actually had a real debate—and then a vote.

Oh, to be fair, Canada did have a debate—a "take note" debate, as they are often called, for at the end of them, no resolution is passed, and no law is written. It is a true replica of a high school debating society, but with lower standards of research and rhetoric. Unlike high school debaters, however, government MPs are allowed only to read pre-approved speeches handed out by the Environment Minister's staff.

Despite the impotent nature of the debate, the time allotted to it was still tightly rationed by the government House Leader—no use wasting time on a pointless exercise. The Prime Minister had already announced that he was going to sign the deal. Why talk about it?

In the U.S. Senate, the opposite was happening. Bill Clinton, the President at the time, was just as pro-Kyoto as Jean Chrétien was. And Al Gore, the Vice President, was even more so—he was the one who compared the threat of global warming to the threat of Adolf Hitler. This is where Chrétien's one-upmanship came from. He saw the U.S. leadership setting the standards for environmental activism.

And so Chrétien declared that at Kyoto he would "beat the U.S."[35] No matter how far Clinton and Gore were willing to go, no matter how deep their emissions reductions would be, Chrétien promised that Canada's would be deeper.

In Canada, Liberal MPs mimicked the Prime Minister in a pointless, non-votable debate.

In the U.S., however, the President and Vice President do not control Congress the way that our Prime Minister controls Parliament. Individual Senators can be immensely powerful—even Senators from states with small populations. Even Senators from states that rely on carbon-based energy.

States such as West Virginia—a state that has been represented by Robert Byrd, the 85-year-old Democrat who was first elected to the Senate in 1958. West Virginia is a tiny state, and its population is actually shrinking—there are barely 1.8 million West Virginians, in a country of 288 million.[36] A lot of West Virginians are coal miners—including Sen. Byrd's late father-in-law. An aging Senator from a tiny state with a declining population and a sprinkling of old coal mines wouldn't carry a lot of clout in most places. But in July of 1997, Sen. Byrd introduced a resolution that forbade the U.S. from agreeing to the Kyoto Protocol, unless developing countries were required to do so too, or if Kyoto "would result in serious harm to the economy of the United States."

What's more, Sen. Byrd's resolution required that any treaty, even ones that met his two criteria, would have to

---

[35] Steven Bernstein and Christopher Gore, "Policy implications of the Kyoto Protocol for Canada," *Isuma*, Winter 2001, p. 31.

[36] U.S. Census Bureau, *Population Division*, December 2002.

be accompanied by a detailed explanation of any legislation or regulatory actions that may be required to implement the protocol...and should also be accompanied by an analysis of the detailed financial costs and other impacts on the economy of the United States which would be incurred by the implementation of the protocol.[37]

That a Senator from a politically incorrect state, representing the politically incorrect coal industry, would have the chutzpah to throw such a straitjacket over a U.S. President—from his own party—is a dramatic display of the strength of the U.S. congressional system, where individual lawmakers can think and act for themselves, and truly represent their own constituents, even if it means contradicting their own party's leader.

That a Senator from a politically incorrect state, representing the politically incorrect coal industry, would have the chutzpah to throw such a straitjacket over a U.S. President—from his own party—is a dramatic display of the strength of the U.S. congressional system.

If only Canada's back-bench government MPs could show such independence. Perhaps we would see Ivan Grose, the Liberal MP from Oshawa, put forward a resolution in Canada's Parliament requiring that his city's auto workers be protected from any taxes and regulations that come with

---

[37] United States Senate Resolution 98, 105th Congress, 1st Session, as agreed to July 15, 1997.

Kyoto. Maybe Stan Keyes, the Liberal MP from Hamilton West, would insist that steel mills in South Korea would face the same emission reductions that those in his own town will face under Kyoto. No such divergence is allowed—even in the meaningless rhetoric of Parliament's "take note" debates on the subject.

Sen. Byrd showed guts *and* smarts. He did not rule out action to control pollution, nor did he even rule out signing Kyoto. He simply drafted a resolution that required all countries to play by the same rules—including Mexico, China, India, Brazil and South Korea, which he strategically mentioned by name. And even if those countries were to sign the same treaty as the U.S. was being asked to sign, Sen. Byrd required that the U.S. government provide a detailed economic plan, proving that the taxes and regulations involved wouldn't hurt the economy. That was the octogenarian Senator's way of saying "just because Mexico's president jumped off a bridge, would you jump off one too?" to Bill Clinton.

Sen. Byrd's resolution was rare for Washington: It was very brief—just 700 words long—and clearly worded. But rarer still was the support Sen. Byrd received from his colleagues.

His resolution was approved unanimously, 95 to 0. Sixty-four Senators liked the resolution so much they asked to be "co-sponsors" of it—so they could take personal credit for it back home in their states.

Barbara Boxer, the ultra-liberal Democrat from California, joined with Sen. Jesse Helms, the arch-conservative Republican from North Carolina. Even Ted Kennedy from Massachusetts signed. So did the late Paul Wellstone, the environmentalist from Minnesota.

Sen. Byrd's resolution in the Senate was the clearest rebuke to Kyoto. But other U.S. lawmakers weren't taking any chances either. Year after year, for example, Michigan Congressman Joe Knollenberg added strict provisos to the U.S. budget, forbidding any bureaucrat from using government money to

> propose or issue rules, regulations, decrees, or orders for the purpose of implementation, or in preparation for implementation, of the Kyoto Protocol[38]

until it is approved by the U.S. Senate—just to be safe.

David Anderson, Canada's Environment Minister, was asked about the wisdom of implementing the Kyoto emissions reductions, if the U.S. wouldn't. Environmentally, the U.S. is the largest emitter of greenhouse gases. And economically, not only is it the world's largest economy, but it is by far Canada's largest trading partner and competitor. Anderson's reply was childlike in its naivete—he said he was just going to hope really hard that the U.S. would change its position. "Well, the first thing I say is that nothing is set in sand," he sputtered, downplaying the significance of the U.S. Senate's bipartisan, unanimous edict. "There is no way in the world that the American position is going to remain as it is,"[39] he said. And, in yet another spectacularly inaccurate prediction, he promised his interviewer,

"There is no way in the world that the American position is going to remain as it is," Anderson said.

---

[38] House Resolution 4635, Department of Veterans Affairs and Housing and Urban Development, and Independent Agencies Appropriations Act, 2001, 106th Congress.

[39] David Anderson, *CBC Radio*, May 18, 2002.

"You're going to see changes in American policy which are quite dramatic, come the November [2002] elections"—a desperate and partisan hope that U.S. voters would somehow replace every single Kyoto skeptic in the Senate. Peppered with more troubling questions, Anderson answered like a scared schoolboy who had run out of answers. "It'll work. Promise you," the grown man and cabinet minister said. It hasn't, of course.

CHAPTER FOUR

Parliament's Most Embarrassing Moment

When a lie—or a simplification, or an exaggeration—is repeated often enough, especially by the media, it takes on the status of the truth. Even when corrections are made, or contrary evidence is put forward, the myth has by then been rechristened as a fact. Like cement, if it is allowed to sit undisturbed for a while, it hardens to rock.

One fascinating example of this was Parliament's debate on global warming in 1997, weeks before the Kyoto convention. A Liberal MP had erroneously stated that the UN scientists were predicting "annual" warming by three to eight degrees Celsius. In fact, the UN's worst-case scenario at that time predicted less than six degrees Celsius of warming over the entire 21st century, not one single year. When Lee Morrison, a Reform MP at the time and an anti-Kyoto skeptic, tried to correct his Liberal colleague he was pounced on like a heretical medieval scientist claiming that the Earth revolved around the Sun.

"I have to categorically reject the suggestion that somehow or other the science is not clear on this issue,"[40] retorted David Pratt, the Liberal who had made the error.

---

[40] David Pratt, *Hansard*, November 26, 1997.

Michelle Dockrill, a New Democrat MP, joined in the inquisition. Did Morrison believe that the whole world was wrong, but he was right? "China agrees with the facts of warming," said Dockrill,[41] employing a novel use of logic. "Does he believe that the Chinese are part of his conspiracy theory?"

Joe Jordan, another Liberal MP, was next in line to ridicule Morrison.

> I am wondering, in the historical context is the member prepared to admit that the earth is round or does he still think it is flat?[42]

Pratt jumped in for another go at things.

> Are all world governments operating with incorrect or faulty scientific information. Is it only the Reform party that has the straight facts on this one?[43]

It was after midnight in Parliament, and besides Morrison, his tormentors and a few back-bench MPs waiting their turn at the microphone, the only people who heard his response were the Speaker of the House, the bilingual translators and some late-night staff. The Liberal cabinet ministers had all long gone home, as did the national press gallery. Too bad; for Morrison's reply was as poignant as it was wise. He said:

> Mr. Speaker, science is not determined by a show of hands. I would answer the honourable member's question with an analogy.[44]

---

[41] Michelle Dockrill, *Hansard*, November 26, 1997.

[42] Joe Jordan, *Hansard*, November 26, 1997.

[43] David Pratt, *Hansard*, November 26, 1997.

[44] Lee Morrison, *Hansard*, November 26, 1997.

If he can recall Copernicus and Galileo, they were thought to be out of their minds. The whole scientific community, the whole bureaucratic community, the whole ecclesiastic community, said these people were mad because they believed that the earth was not the centre of the universe, that in fact the earth and the planets rotated around the Sun. They received much the same treatment that some of your eminent climatologists today are receiving from the herd when they speak out against a theory which they say, in their opinion, is not proven.

The bravura speech of the evening was made before a fuller House of Commons and a sprinkling of reporters in the press gallery, but for all it was heeded it could have been delivered at midnight, along with Morrison's. Preston Manning, then the Leader of the Opposition, had spent weeks sifting through scientific studies and economic reports—and had asked close to 100 questions of the government in the daily Question Period. His criticisms, leveled in 1997, are often word-for-word the criticisms being posited today. In part, that is because Manning's concern about Kyoto stemmed from the fact that he had been one of the few Parliamentarians to spend any time doing some investigations into the subject, before Chrétien announced his intentions to ratify the deal in the fall of 2002. But the main reason why so many of Manning's points are still relevant today is that the government has yet to answer his questions, five years after they were first put.[45] He said:

> The minister has yet to lay before the House a definitive statement of the economic, sectoral, regional and taxpayer impacts of pursuing its CO_2 emissions reduction targets.

---

[45] Preston Manning, *Hansard*, November 26, 1997.

Those impact assessments are still wanting. Also:

> The minister has yet to satisfy the House that the government has a workable agreement with the provinces or with anyone else for achieving its targets and paying the bills.

Five years later provincial discord is only growing. Manning challenged the government's use of science—and pointed out that Ottawa had a troubling habit of twisting empirical data to fit political agendas. He noted:

> I refer particularly to the record of this government and the previous government in bringing science to bear on the sustaining of the fisheries, particularly the Atlantic fishery.

Manning bruited a theory of his own: that dozens of politicians and diplomats, crammed into a room in an isolated, faraway convention hall, given an artificial deadline to draft a treaty, and placed in the scrutiny of the media fishbowl, would sign any deal, no matter how flawed. He called it the "Meech Lake effect" and said:

> It was in full operation at the Rio summit in 1992 where over 100 world leaders met in isolation from their publics for almost a week with almost 9,000 media people panting for an instant, simplistic solution to a complex problem.

> Where is the economic impact assessment that supports the job creation and economic activity that are associated with new technologies and exporting to which the minister referred?

> Where is the assessment that indicates the value of that activity would come even remotely close to compensating for the job loss and curtailment of economic activity required to reduce CO_2 emissions to 1990 levels?

Where is the assessment from the transportation minister?

Where is the assessment of the trade minister on the trade impacts?

Where are the assessments of the so-called regional development ministers on the impacts on the West, Ontario, Quebec, the Atlantic region and the North?

In his desire to be seen as a good green fellow at international environmental gatherings, he seems to have forgotten where he lives and whom he represents....He is not the Prime Minister of a unitary state...he is not the Prime Minister of Fiji where they can survive without much extra energy....He needs to be reminded that he is not the Prime Minister of Belgium, a small country that can be driven across in a few hours. He is the Prime Minister of the second largest country in the world, a northern exporting country of immense distances that has an energy requirement for transportation, an energy requirement for heating just for survival, an energy requirement for manufacturing and processing that is particular to this country and requires a particularized approach to CO_2 emission limits.

But the days when a passionate, informed parliamentary speech could change minds and sway votes are days long gone. Few government MPs heard Manning's speech; and if they were at all moved by it, they long ago lost the practice of voting their own minds, substituting instead the party whip's instructions for their own judgment.

CHAPTER FIVE

Disguised Foreign Aid

So how does Kyoto work? What does it say?

It is true that Kyoto is an environmental treaty—but that is only part of the story. Kyoto requires industrialized nations to reduce their emissions of gases such as carbon dioxide, which are the natural by-products of everything from farming to driving to steel-making. But because the reductions called for under Kyoto are so drastic, it would be impossible to meet Kyoto's targets simply through energy efficiency or other tinkering. By the time Canada reaches Kyoto's deadline, in 2012, we will be emitting 30 per cent more greenhouse gases than we are permitted—a function of population growth and economic growth. Unless we plan on literally banning millions of cars from the road and shutting down hundreds of factories, there is no way to meet the targets through cuts alone. Energy is the lifeblood of a modern economy; to reduce our energy use by 30 per cent is to reduce our standard of living by 30 per cent—to become a permanently poor nation.

The architects of Kyoto know this. And while they do indeed hope that countries such as Canada will reduce emissions, they have put a safety valve in the treaty. If a "wealthy" country such as Canada can't stay within its Kyoto emissions quota, it can buy the right to produce more emissions, from other, poorer countries.

Article 12 of Kyoto allows countries such as Canada to buy environmental forgiveness if we can't reduce our emissions, by spending money building power plants or other "clean" industries in the Third World. It's called the Clean Development Mechanism, and it's one of Kyoto's fudge-factors. It does not reduce greenhouse gases at all; in fact, the economic activity inherent in any economic development probably increases the emissions of greenhouse gases. It's foreign aid for foreign development, done under the politically expedient cloak of environmental correctness.

Another fudge-factor in Kyoto is Article 6. If countries such as Canada can't stay within the Kyoto emissions quota, and don't want to spend money developing someone else's economy, Article 6 allows Canada to make an outright gift of money—skeptics would call it a fine, or a bribe—to be exempted. The payment would go straight to countries who have not used up their Kyoto emissions quota, such as Russia and the Ukraine, to name two.

This is a gift, the purest definition of foreign aid.

This is a gift; the purest definition of foreign aid. Canadians who pay the money—whether taxpayers, because the federal government makes the payment, or consumers, because a company makes the payment—get nothing real in return. Canada would acquire imaginary "permits" or "credits" or "quotas" to use more energy and emit more carbon dioxide. But Canada and all other nations already have that right; certainly Russia does not have sovereignty over Canadian citizens. But the fiction is needed, as fiction is employed in so many other aspects of the entire Kyoto debate.

While most Canadians who are engaged in the Kyoto discussion focus on the impossibility of taking carbon out of our economy, or on the dubious nature of the science of global warming, very few have seen Kyoto for what it is: Maurice Strong's hidden transfer of wealth from industrialized countries such as Canada to poor—and often corrupt—countries in the Third World.

THE KYOTO ACCORD IS A TRADE AGREEMENT

Aldyen Donnelly is one of the few Canadians who see Kyoto as an economic deal first, and an environmental deal second. She says:

> The Kyoto Accord is a trade agreement, and it's an agreement that was designed by some of its core authors to effect the transfer of wealth from energy exporting nations to energy importing nations.[46]

Donnelly is the president of Vancouver's Greenhouse Emission Management Consortium—a group of companies that are gearing up for the business of emissions trading. "The Kyoto Protocol assigns to the participating nations a national quota, and that quota is tradable." Donnelly's group plans to trade—using taxpayers' money, customers' money, or both. It's a business built on buying and selling imaginary "credits" and "rights." It would make the wild dot-com investments of the late 1990s—where companies with no revenues and high losses were hugely overvalued— look responsible by comparison. At least dot-coms did something. Buying the right to emit carbon dioxide—and buying that right from a foreign country—wouldn't pass the

---

[46] Aldyen Donnelly, *CBC Radio*, May 28, 2002.

Enron smell test. But Kyoto isn't a company governed by securities laws; it's a foreign treaty, built on guilt, hype and politics.

Donnelly points out that within Canada's allowable Kyoto target—fixed at six per cent less than the level of carbon we were emitting in 1990—Canada can do whatever we like. We can use up our carbon quota by farming, or driving, or breathing, or heating our homes, in whatever combination we like. But in 2012 when Kyoto's deadline kicks in, once we reach our limit—571 megatonnes[47]—then we either have to stop our economy, or pay up. Given Canada's current trends, by 2012 we will be burning through our 517 megatonnes by mid-September. Either we all park our cars and turn off our furnaces for the rest of the year, or we pay the fines.

In 2012 when Kyoto's deadline kicks in, once we reach our limit we either have to stop our economy, or pay up.

Donnelly puts it a slightly different way:

> The quota governs each nation's right to do the following things in combination: produce fossil fuels, plus produce beef, pork and rice, plus produce pulp and paper. So if we ratified the treaty and it went into full effect, from the day it's in effect forward, we cannot increase, for example, our export of energy to the United States without reducing either our domestic consumption of fossil fuels or production of beef, or pork, or rice, or paper, or tissue.

A nation's economic strength, then, is determined by its

---

[47] "A Discussion Paper on Canada's Contribution to Addressing Climate Change," Government of Canada, Ottawa, 2002, p. 15.

emissions quota. Russia and other former Soviet Bloc countries were given massive quota surpluses; the United States was given the largest quota, but still far less than they use each year. Thus, says Donnelly:

> The effect of the agreement is that nations that hold the largest supplies of quota end up having the greatest control of the global market.

Kyoto puts literally any country in the world in a position to demand payment from Canadians, to give us their assent to use energy.

All of this is just make-believe right now. Canadians don't need anybody's permission before buying a litre of gas, or exhaling an ounce of carbon dioxide. It will be a shocking change, though, once every emission uses up a pound of quota here, a megatonne there. That's where Donnelly's company comes in. Quota holders

> win as soon as they get the quota regime in place...we've transferred a certain amount of sovereignty over economic activities to those who hold the greatest supply of quota when we sign the treaty.

Donnelly's right—once we burn through our 571 megatonnes, we are at the mercy of foreign countries to sell us their extra carbon permission.

So where is Maude Barlow and the Council of Canadians? During the great free trade debates, they railed against handing over the economic levers of our country to foreigners—specifically, the United States, and then to Mexico. But Kyoto puts literally any country in the world in a position to demand payment from Canadians, to give us their assent to use energy. At the recent UN Summit in Johannesburg, Barlow complained that "Kyoto is only one example of the business-led opposition to real sustainable development."[48] It's nice that Barlow has a side interest in the environment. But where is she on her number one pet peeve—the loss of Canadian economic sovereignty?

Like everything, the price of Kyoto credits will depend on supply and demand. If a dozen different countries are desperately behind on their emission cutbacks, but only one country has a Kyoto surplus, the price could be quite high. Alternatively, a group of Third World countries, each with surplus quotas to sell, could band together in an OPEC-style cartel of carbon dioxide. It's a strong analogy: The West needs oil to run our cars and factories and heat our homes. Under Kyoto, we won't just need to buy oil—we'll need to buy permission to burn that oil.

> It's nice that Maude Barlow has a side interest in the environment. Where is she on her number one pet peeve—the loss of Canadian economic sovereignty?

How would a Third World country know how much of its quota it has left to sell? How would a country such as Canada know how much it could buy from another country? How would they measure? When countries buy and sell real things—like cars, or barrels of oil—the question does not arise; buyers and sellers simply count the number of units produced, shipped and received. But what is to stop a Third World country—desperate for cash—from simply pretending that it has extra Kyoto quota to sell? And, even if the buying country knows that the selling country is cheating, since it's all an accounting shell game

---

[48] Council of Canadians, "A Canadian Injured as Protest is Crushed by Police in Johannesburg," Ottawa, August 24, 2002.

anyway, what is to stop an industrial country—desperate for the right to keep using energy—from going along with the ruse? Measuring carbon dioxide emissions is itself largely based on guesswork and assumptions—especially in remote, large or technologically backward countries, which partly describes Russia. Measuring the invisible rights to invisible carbon dioxide—well, that invites a whole new level of creative accounting.

EMISSION CREDITS AS NEW PROPERTY

Murray Sayle, an analyst who is sympathetic to Kyoto, says the treaty "created a new form of property—emission permits—worth over $2-trillion."[49] That property, of course, is actually worthless; you can't eat a Kyoto credit, you can't fuel your car with one. It's fairy dust, but the UN says it's real. Says Sayle:

> If emission trading ever happens, Russia and the Ukraine could collect between $12-$170-billion between 2008 and 2012, perhaps more, by selling the results of their industrial decline to the Western nations depending on how the more successful countries get on with their targets, and this without making any real reductions at all...

> What Kyoto tactfully calls the "reforming countries" have seen their heavy industries collapse, and are 0.6 per cent down on 1990 levels—or, put another way, these countries could have 6.3-billion tons of emission rights to sell.[50]

Kyoto's emissions trading doesn't just let industrial

---

[49]Murray Sayle, "After George W. Bush, the Deluge," *London Review of Books*, Vol. 23 No. 12, June 21, 2001.

[50] Sayle, 2001.

countries off the hook. It rewards countries such as Russia and the former East Germany for being extraordinarily filthy in 1990, the year the standards were set. By contrast, Canada—clean, and with a growing population and economy—is punished.

The Russians know this; they smile when solipsistic activists such as David Suzuki hail Kyoto as an environmental treaty, rather than a foreign aid treaty. A recent article in *Pravda* scoffs at the science behind Kyoto, but rejoices in its economics:

> Russia's carbon dioxide emission in 1990 was maximum. It made up 540 million tons. Nowadays, Russia emits 400 million tons. Thus, there is an opportunity to talk about selling the quotas for the emission of industrial gases for $30-$50 per ton.[51]

If *Pravda's* analysis is correct, Russia will profit $4.2-billion to $7-billion each year—on the low end of Sayle's 2001 prediction.

Russia's profits won't come from anything Russia has produced, but rather from the imaginary credits that countries such as Canada will buy from them. And in Canada's draft Kyoto plan, the federal government has budgeted for a minimum yearly purchase of 55 million tonnes of credits.[52]

We won't know how much Canada's planned 55 million tonnes of credits will cost, until Kyoto takes effect and the imaginary trading begins in earnest; right now, only a handful

---

[51] Andrey Mikhailov, "Kyoto Protocol Not Worth a Thing, *Pravda*, October 19, 2002 translated by Dmitry Sudakov.

[52] *Climate Change Draft Plan*, Government of Canada, 2002, p. 17.

of energy companies trade in carbon credits, in small amounts and largely for public relations value. Rich Rosenweig, a spokesman for a carbon-trading company called Natsource, says that prices are already at US $16 per tonne[53]—not too far off *Pravda's* predicted price—which would put Canada's annual emission trading tab at $1.32-billion Canadian dollars. Of course, if Canada placed such a huge order, the world price of imaginary credits would likely rise—and, of course, other quota-thirsty countries might enter the market en masse.

Emissions trading is a fancy way of dressing up foreign aid to the Third World—Maurice Strong's $125-billion quiet transfer of wealth. But Strong didn't ignore the unquenchable thirst that Canadian politicians have for tax dollars, either. In 1999 Strong said:

Emissions trading is a fancy way of dressing up foreign aid to the Third World.

I think it is inevitable that we move to a carbon tax of some kind…What today may seem totally unrealistic will become inevitable tomorrow…

If we do not accelerate the measure we have taken, somewhat tepidly so far, we won't make it. That will be a serious embarrassment for Canada.[54]

When asked about Strong's comments, Ralph Goodale, the Natural Resources Minister at the time, answered:

A carbon tax is not a part of our planning or our

---

[53] Julie Vorman, "Global carbon credit market seen tripling this year," *Reuters*, October 18, 2002.

[54] Sheldon Alberts, "Carbon tax 'inevitable' to slash emissions: Strong," *National Post*, May 20, 1999, p. A4.

thinking. Our whole orientation is to relieve the tax burden, not increase the tax burden.

Two years later, however, the Environment Department was paying bureaucrats to draft up proposals for a 50-cent-per-litre gasoline tax, and up to a 100 per cent jump in the price of home heating.[55]

From foreign aid to buying and selling imaginary credits, Kyoto is as much a treaty about taxes and trade as it is about the environment.

---

[55] Mark Jaccard, "Costing Greenhouse Gas Abatement," *Isuma*, Winter 2001.

CHAPTER SIX

The Intergovernmental Panel on Climate Change

It is not acceptable in polite company to dispute the science of Kyoto—to do so is not just considered unfashionable, but deeply offensive. Even in no-holds-barred debates where there is supposed to be dissent, Kyoto skeptics are treated like heretics who ought to be silenced, not reasoned with or appealed to. The Kyoto taboo seems unbreakable.

The science of Kyoto is not questioned. Oddly, though, any superstition that adds to the Kyoto myth is tacked on the body of science without hesitation, every newsworthy weather event—including cold spells—is immediately christened as yet more irrefutable proof of global warming.

After all, "thousands" of scientists have declared that global warming exists, so any rejection of Kyoto's academic pedigree is about as politically correct as denying Darwin's Theory of Evolution. Even Alberta Premier Ralph Klein, an opponent of Kyoto who made a public relations decision not to challenge the science behind Kyoto, has been tagged a political Neanderthal[56] by the Liberal party. Apparently, opposing the political and economic solutions hammered out by UN diplomats now carries the same opprobrium as challenging the science itself.

---

[56] "Ontario critic paints Klein as a 'Neanderthal'," *Calgary Herald*, October 17, 2002, p. A5.

But why can't the science of Kyoto be challenged? After all, if the evidence is indeed conclusive, wouldn't Kyoto's promoters be happy to have skeptics pore over the proof—like heathens demanding to see the Bible? Shouldn't Kyoto's fundamentalists—so certain are they of their righteousness—be inviting heretics to study Kyoto's holy books?

There are reasons why Kyoto's fanatics react so viscerally to any challenge to the science. For one thing, most Kyoto boosters haven't actually read the scientific background themselves—they have taken it on faith, and when faced with a doubter, they are publicly confronted with the possibility that they have been fooled—a terrifying and embarrassing thought. During Canada's heated free trade debate in the 1980s, the most embarrassing moment was when John Crosbie, the Trade Minister, admitted that he had not read the entire Free Trade Agreement that he himself had proposed as a parliamentary law.

The science behind Kyoto is suspect at best—and rooted in political and environmental fraud at worst.

Does anyone truly believe that the Prime Minister has muscled through the dozens of pages of dense legalese that comprises the Kyoto Protocol, let alone the hundreds of pages of scientific studies claiming that Kyoto is even necessary?

But for those pro-Kyoto activists who actually have read the science, there is a much deeper reason to scare off would-be inspectors. And that is, the science behind Kyoto is suspect at best—and rooted in political and environmental fraud at worst.

THE IPCC WORKING GROUPS

The world's largest study on global warming was conducted by the UN's Intergovernmental Panel on Climate Change—or IPCC for short. The IPCC was set up in 1988, with three working groups. Working Group 1's job was to study whether or not there really was global warming—and whether or not human activity had anything to do with it. That group was made up largely of climate scientists. Working Group 2 was a mix of different scientific disciplines, whose job was to predict what the impact would be if, indeed, global warming was happening. And Working Group 3 was another mixed group of scientists, whose job it was to brainstorm ways to deal with the impact of any global warming.[57]

These working groups consisted of hundreds of scientists, some of whom actually drafted the scientific reports—called "lead writers"—and some of whom reviewed the studies, using the scientific rules of inquiry.

The IPCC reports were designed to be the basis for Kyoto—they were supposed to be the authoritative, scientific proof that politicians had to act. Without the impartial pedigree of the IPCC, Kyotocrats would be seen as nothing more than international busy-bodies, pursuing their own agendas. But flash a report loaded with plenty of PhDs' signatures and packed with scientific jargon, and the Kyotocrats would be transformed into selfless servants of the planet, acting on a solid scientific warning.

---

[57] John Lanchbery and David Victor, "The Role of Science in the Global Climate Negotiations," in Helge Ole Bergesen, Georg Parmann, and Oystein B. Thommessen (eds.), *Green Globe Yearbook of International Co-operation on Environment and Development*, Oxford University Press, 1995, p. 33.

Working Groups 2 and 3 were never as important as Working Group 1—because what WG1 reported would determine whether or not the whole Kyoto process would proceed. There is not much point studying the impact of global warming or coming up with responses to it, if the WG1 scientists declared that the Earth wasn't warming, or that it was, but humans weren't causing it.

The original WG1 report was approved by the IPCC scientists in December 1995—it was "peer reviewed" by scientists in an open debate, who all signed off on the final draft. But after the IPCC had finished circulating the report, they made further changes—changes that came as a shock to many of the IPCC scientists in WG1, who had signed their names to the report. When the UN released the final paper in May 1996, it had doctored the study, without asking permission of its authors or even consulting them.

IPCC CONCLUSIONS INVENTED

Secretly editing the IPCC report is more than just dirty politics. It's a violation of the entire ethical basis of science, which, in contrast to political spin and propaganda, is supposed to be a practice of open, methodical discussion in search of the truth, wherever it may lie. The doctored IPCC report deliberately downplayed the WG1 scientists' doubts about global warming, in order to conform to the UN's political agenda.

As Dr. Frederick Seitz, wrote in *The Wall Street Journal*:

> In my more than 60 years as a member of the American scientific community, including service as president of both the National Academy of Sciences and the American Physical Society, I have never witnessed a

more disturbing corruption of the peer-review process than the events that led to this IPCC report.[58]

Dr. Seitz is no crank; in addition to being past president of America's two leading scientific academies, he was the president emeritus of Rockefeller University and chairman of the George C. Marshall Institute when he wrote his scorching letter. According to Dr. Seitz:

> More than 15 sections in Chapter 8 of the report—the key chapter setting out the scientific evidence for and against a human influence over climate—were changed or deleted after the scientists charged with examining this question had accepted the supposedly final text.

These changes were not simply correcting spelling errors or formatting the pages, he noted.

As Dr. Frederick Seitz, wrote in *The Wall Street Journal:* "In my more than 60 years as a member of the American scientific community, including service as president of both the National Academy of Sciences and the American Physical Society, I have never witnessed a more disturbing corruption of the peer-review process than the events that led to this IPCC report."

Few of these changes were merely cosmetic; nearly all worked to remove hints of the skepticism with which many scientists regard claims that human activities are having a major impact on climate in general and on global warming in particular.

---

58 Frederick Seitz, "A Major Deception on Global Warming," *The Wall Street Journal*, June 12, 1996.

Dr. Seitz isn't the only scientist who is appalled at the way the UN twisted the IPCC results to get the political answers they were looking for. Dr. Fred Singer of Arlington, Virginia's Science and Environmental Policy Project has gone through the IPCC report line by line, showing how a lot of scientific "maybes" were changed to political "for sures." Like Dr. Seitz, Dr. Singer is no slouch. An atmospheric physicist, his credentials include professor emeritus of environmental science at the University of Virginia, and his track record includes being the first director of the U.S. Weather Satellite Service.

Dr. Singer obtained the scientifically approved copy of the WG1 report, and compared it to the doctored version.[59] Section 8.1 is a typical example of the fraud. The original version of this paragraph of the report reads like this:

> The attribution of a detected climate change to a particular causal mechanism can be established only by testing of competing hypotheses.

Translation: We don't have any proof that global warming is caused by people—to find out for sure, we will have to do "testing" first.

The doctored version that was published, however, reads like this:

> The attribution of a detected climate change to a particular causal mechanism involves tests of competing hypotheses.

Translation: blaming humans for global warming is based on tests.

---

[59] Dr. Fred S. Singer, The IPCC Controversy, Item 3. On-line posting. The Science and Environmental Policy Project. <http://www.sepp.org>

The original version says that blaming people can "only" be done after doing more tests in the future.

The doctored version removes the future tense completely, blames people and invokes "tests" that have not yet even occurred.

Another similar change was made in section 8.2.5. In that section, IPCC scientists originally wrote that "current" work to measure global warming "has not attempted to account for these...uncertainties." The doctored version is a flat-out lie. It says that "current" work "is now beginning to account for these...uncertainties." But it isn't. And the scientists said so. But the UN bosses knew what they had to do.

Perhaps the most stark example of IPCC censoring is section 8.6 of the WG1 report. The original version, approved by the scientists, started off with this blunt admission:

> Finally we come to the most difficult question of all: "When will the detection and unambiguous attribution of human-induced climate change occur?" In the light of the very large...uncertainties discussed in this Chapter, it is not surprising that the best answer to this question is "We do not know."

The scientists were clear. They said given the "very large" uncertainties, they could not, as scientists, take a position that humans cause global warming.

But had that sentence been allowed to see the light of day, the entire momentum of the global warming freight train would have been derailed. So this is the version that the IPCC actually published:

> Finally we come to the difficult question of when the detection and attribution of human-included climate change is likely to occur. The answer to this question

must be subjective, particularly in the light of the very large...uncertainties discussed in this Chapter.

The scientists' "most difficult question" is now just a "difficult question"—when will proof of human blame for global warming be found? But in the censors' version of that question, the word "unambiguous" is dropped—any proof of human blame, even subjective, opinionated, uncertain proof, is now all that the IPCC bosses claim they were ever looking for.

And instead of providing the scientists answer—"We do not know"—the IPCC continues on to say that, indeed, it does know. Without checking with anyone, the IPCC added the following statement—180-degrees opposite of the scientists' conclusions: "The body of statistical evidence...now points toward discernible human influence on global climate."

That was not the view of hundreds of climate scientists. That was not the conclusion that the peer-reviewed report came to. The "most difficult question" of human involvement came back with a pretty frank answer: "We do not know." It was written right in section 8.6 of the IPCC's own report.

But you can't sign a treaty based on a scientific "do not know." So it was changed. Dr. Singer and other scientists blew the whistle on the IPCC fraud, and they did get some media coverage. But long after their protests stopped echoing in newspapers, the IPCC studies continue to be cited with great authority by politicians and the media alike. Most pro-Kyoto diplomats, politicians and media probably are not aware of the editing fraud within. Unfortunately, even if they were aware of the fraud, few would probably stop citing them. That's because Kyoto isn't about science. It's about a view of the world that condemns industry and commerce—facts be damned.

That one, fabricated sentence from the IPCC report is often the only sentence that journalists covering Kyoto have even heard of. In a massive review of Kyoto in the *London Review of Books*, journalist Murray Sayle writes, "What concentrated minds at Kyoto was a single sentence in the IPCC's...Report of 1995"—and then he quotes, verbatim, the fabricated sentence about "discernible human influence on global climate." Of course Sayle believed the report was

That's because Kyoto isn't about science. It's about a view of the world that condemns industry and commerce—facts be damned.

true. "As far as any humans can be," he wrote, "the IPCC's scientists are as impartial as the air we breathe."[60] He calls them a "star-studded panel." That may be true about the scientists, but apparently Sayle hadn't met the IPCC's editors, at UN headquarters.

KYOTO'S CRITICS AND KYOTO'S APOLOGISTS

Even the most skeptical Kyoto critics have been fooled by that fabricated sentence—and are left to try to massage it, or counter it. One of the best Canadian rebuttals to Kyoto was a scathing critique compiled by Laura Jones, the former Environmental Economist at Vancouver's prestigious Fraser Institute. But even Jones quotes that fabricated IPCC sentence—alleging a "discernable human influence on

---

[60] Murray Sayle, "After George W. Bush, the Deluge," *London Review of Books*, Vol. 23 No. 12, June 21, 2001.

climate"—as the case she and other Kyoto skeptics have to meet.[61] Jones and other academic analysts have made the mistake of assuming that the UN report was written with the same academic integrity with which Jones and others approached the subject.

Rather than denying the stunning accusations made by Dr. Seitz, Dr. Singer and others, the UN's point-men on the report justified them. IPCC chairman Bert Bolin, along with the co-chairs of Working Group 1, excused their eleventh-hour edits by pointing out that U.S. President Bill Clinton's diplomat in charge of reviewing the report demanded that "the chapter authors be prevailed upon to modify their text in an appropriate manner."[62] Dr. Stephen Schneider, an IPCC Working Group 1 member and a global warming believer, published a lengthy defence of document-doctoring, pointing out:

> A careful reading of the IPCC's formal rules reveals that in fact the rules *neither allow nor prohibit* changes to a report after its formal acceptance.

The italics are Dr. Schneider's own emphasis. That is the IPCC's excuse—a lawyer's hair-splitting search for a logical loophole to justify twisting science. Doctoring documents isn't permitted, says the IPCC, but it isn't specifically ruled out. That is not a denial of a cover-up—it is a depressing explanation.

The IPCC's defenders are philosophical about abandoning their objectivity for their new role as propagandists.

---

[61] *Global Warming*, Edited by Laura Jones, The Fraser Institute, 1997, p. 6.

[62] Paul N. Edwards, Stephen H. Schneider, "The 1995 IPCC Report: Broad Consensus or 'Scientific Cleansing'?," *Ecofable/Ecoscience* 1:1 1997, pp. 3-9.

In Dr. Schneider's lengthy excuse for the cover-up, he explains why the IPCC had to do it:

> Occasionally, non-conventional outlier opinions revolutionize scientific dogma (Galileo and Einstein being the most oft-cited examples).

But, according to Dr. Schneider, "the general public cannot be relied upon to determine for themselves how to weigh these conflicting opinions." That has to be left to self-appointed scientific censors such as Dr. Schneider and the other IPCC scientists who knew what their real job was: Get proof of human-caused global warming, even if it takes the scientific equivalent of Watergate. "This kind of consensus is not the same thing as 'truth'," admitted Dr. Schneider.[63] Actually, there is neither truth nor consensus in the Kyoto "science."

The scientific censors knew what their real job was: get proof of human-caused global warming, even if it takes the scientific equivalent of Watergate.

(Dr. Schneider seems quite eager to bend his science to suit political and media fashions. In 1976, he called the science of global cooling "compelling" and praised a fearmongering book, *The Cooling: Has the next ice age begun? Can we survive it?*, calling it a "good place to start.")[64]

The 1996 IPCC fraud—strategically timed to land before the 1997 Kyoto conference—was not the first time that genuine scientists had been used to camouflage the

---

63 Paul N. Edwards, Stephen H. Schneider, pp. 3-9.

64 Richard S. Lindzen, "A Contrarian Voice," *Regulation*, Spring, 1998, p. 68.

decidedly unscientific objectives of UN diplomats on the eve of a convention. In the run-up to the 1992 Rio conference, the IPCC released a scientific report then, too. Like the jiggery-pokery in the 1996 report, the IPCC wrote a politicized "policy-makers summary" of the 365-page study in 1990. Dr. Singer surveyed the U.S. scientists who participated in writing that report—both as contributors and peer-reviewers—and found that there was "no scientific consensus backing the IPCC conclusions."[65] According to Dr. Singer, "the IPCC Policy-makers Summary is essentially a political document, not a scientific document. It was prepared for and agreed to by the government representatives to the Intergovernmental Panel on Climate Change, and influenced by accredited delegates from other organizations, including environmental pressure groups," said Dr. Singer.

"Policy-makers," of course, is a euphemism for politicians. And though the politicians have never formally had a role in drafting IPCC documents, they have always reserved unto themselves the last edit of the IPCC's work. In the wake of Dr. Seitz's 1996 accusations, an unnamed IPCC official told *Nature* magazine that the scientists' work was revised "to ensure that it conformed to a 'policy-makers' summary' of the full report."[66] But shouldn't a "summary" of a scientific report be written to conform to that report? How can a truly scientific report be forced to conform to a fixed political outcome? In boxing, that's calling rigging the fight.

---

[65] "Panel Questions IPCC Analysis: scientists find discrepancies in global warming," *Eco-Logic*, August 1992, p. 8.

[66] "Climate Debate Must not Overheat," *Nature* 381 (6583), June 13, 1996, p. 539.

In the decade since the first instances of report-rigging by the UN, hundreds of scientists—including many who were involved with the IPCC—have decided that, to save the reputation of science, they have to denounce the obvious political hijacking that has been going on. These scientists have signed a mass declaration, stating "we consider the scientific basis of the 1992 Global Climate Treaty to be flawed and its goal to be unrealistic."[67] Among them are Dr. Robert Balling, Dr. Anthony Lupo and Dr. Patrick Michaels—all official IPCC reviewers or contributors, all disillusioned with being used simply for credential camouflage.

Another 17,000 scientists from other related disciplines have signed a petition[68] against Kyoto, stating:

> The proposed limits on greenhouse gases would harm the environment, hinder the advance of science and technology, and damage the health and welfare of mankind.

Their rationale?

> There is no convincing scientific evidence that human release of carbon dioxide, methane, or other greenhouse gases is causing or will, in the foreseeable future, cause catastrophic heating of the Earth's atmosphere and disruption of the Earth's climate. Moreover, there is substantial scientific evidence that increases in atmospheric carbon dioxide produce many beneficial effects upon the natural plant and animal environments of the Earth.

---

[67] "The Leipzig Declaration," *International Symposium on the Greenhouse Controversy*, Nov. 9-10, 1995.

[68] Douglas Houts, "SEPP News release," April 20, 1998. On-line posting. The Science and Environmental Policy Project. <http://www.sepp.org>

Of course, scientific facts cannot be determined through a vote, or by counting signatures on a petition. But the dissent of so many scientists, especially those intimately involved with the UN's studies, should raise alarm bells. It seems to have done so: By mid-November 2002, an Environics poll[69] showed that only 20 per cent of Canadians "believe that the science upon which the foundation of Kyoto is based on has been settled"; fully 74 per cent of Canadians wanted to hear from non-government scientists on the subject. They simply don't believe the hype.

The dissent of so many scientists, especially those intimately involved with the UN's studies, should raise alarm bells.

DOCTORED DATA

The IPCC has continued to study the science of global warming—and the academic conclusions of scientists have continued to be edited in the final reports by Kyotocrats back at UN headquarters.

Dr. Michaels, a University of Virginia climatologist who served on the IPCC, says more than just political spin was added to the scientific reports. Actual data was doctored. For example, the report's worst-case, extreme scenario claimed that the maximum temperature rise of the next century would be six degrees Celsius. "But the doc-

---

69 Environics Research Group, "Environics poll reveals that majority of Canadians unconvinced about science of Kyoto, support further consultations prior to ratification of Accord," News release, November 14, 2002.

ument the IPCC sent out for scientific peer review contained no such number," says Dr. Michaels. "Indeed, after the scientists reviewed it, the maximum value was 4.8 degrees (Celsius)." This change was made "*after* the document had circulated among scientific reviewers," he says. The IPCC inserted the report's most shocking conclusion "at the 11th hour, after the scientific peer review process had concluded."[70]

Dr. John Christy is another scientist who worked on several reports for IPCC, rising to the rank of a "lead author" for the IPCC in 2001. A PhD in Climate Dynamics and the winner of the NASA Medal for Exceptional Scientific Achievement, Dr. Christy recently published an insider's expose of junk science masquerading as independent research. It's unlikely that he'll be invited back to work on the next IPCC report.

Dr. Christy's scathing exposé is so effective because he is completely unemotional about his science—he reports facts as he finds them, not how he wants them to be. One by one, he demolishes the media myths about global warming—starting with the myth that the IPCC scientists all agree with the UN's findings. In fact, each group of scientists worked on only their own part of the report. He said:

> Statements by ideological environmentalists that thousands of IPCC scientists agree on anything is simply untrue and misrepresents the process.

And the summary of the report—the "dumbed-down" version sent to journalists?

---

[70] On-line posting. Global Warming Information Page. <http://www.globalwarming.org>

> Though drafted by a small group of IPCC scientists, the brief account of the main points used by the media and called the Summary for Policy-makers, was actually edited and approved by a political body.[71]

That should be enough to sow seeds of doubt with anyone.

---

[71] John Christy, "The Global Warming Fiasco," *Global Warming and Other Eco-Myths*, edited by Ronald Bailey, Competitive Enterprise Institute, 2002, p. 7.

CHAPTER SEVEN

The Truth About Carbon Dioxide

Thank God for global warming and the greenhouse effect. Really. Without it, the Earth would be 33 degrees Celsius colder than it is—the whole planet would be frozen.[72]

Gases in our atmosphere let the Sun's light and energy into the Earth's atmosphere, but they won't let that energy back out. That's why it's called the greenhouse effect. The vast majority of heat-trapping greenhouse gases—far more than 99 per cent—occur in nature: Water vapour being the main one, carbon dioxide and methane being the next most common. There are a handful of other extremely rare gases, such as sulphur hexafluoride and perfluorocarbons,[73] which trap heat, too.

CARBON DIOXIDE IS NOT A POLLUTANT

Carbon dioxide, the main greenhouse gas targeted by Kyoto, isn't poisonous. In fact, the opposite is true: Carbon dioxide is essential for life on Earth. It is the crucial gas needed for plant life—anything green requires carbon

---

[72] U.S. Environmental Protection Agency, "Greenhouse Gases and Global Warming Potential Values," excerpt from the *Inventory of U.S. Greenhouse Emissions and Sinks: 1990-2000*, April, 2002, p. 3.

[73] U.S. Environmental Protection Agency, pp. 5-7.

dioxide to grow. Humans and animals inhale oxygen—what plants emit—and exhale carbon dioxide. Call it the circle of life.

Carbon dioxide is quite scarce in the environment, making up only 0.037 per cent of air, or 369 parts per million.[74]

But more than 95 per cent of all carbon dioxide emitted into the atmosphere comes from natural sources,[75] including the world's oceans, decaying vegetation and animal breathing—and then there's the massive methane emissions from animals. All told, 210,000 megatonnes of CO_2 are released every year in nature—in addition to natural sources of methane. By contrast, the entire planet's man-made carbon dioxide emissions from all economic activity amounts to just 6,300 megatonnes.[76] Whether or not Canada cuts back its 240 Kyoto megatonnes of CO_2 and other greenhouse gases will make a great deal of difference to our standard of living and our daily routines; but it will reduce carbon dioxide in the atmosphere by about one tenth of a per cent—until our non-Kyoto competitors in the U.S., China and India cancel us out.

Dr. Tom Wigley, one of the lead authors of the IPCC report, estimates that even if the human-generated global warming theory is true, and even if every country fulfilled

---

[74] Climate Change 2001, *Intergovernmental Panel on Climate Change*, 2001, Appendix II.

[75] John Christy, "The Global Warming Fiasco," *Global Warming and Other Eco-Myths*, edited by Ronald Bailey, Competitive Enterprise Institute, 2002, p. 10.

[76] John Christy, personal interview, November 15, 2002.

its Kyoto requirements, by the end of the 21st century, the impact on the climate would be trivial—the world would be 1.9 degrees Celsius hotter, rather than 2.1 degrees Celsius. In other words, the global temperature that would normally be reached by the year 2094 would be delayed until 2100—a century's worth of economic rationing, to delay a 0.2 degree warming trend by six years.[77] Even if the UN theory is correct, what's the point?

Some Kyoto fanatics believe that we should implement the treaty anyway, and that even if one hundred other countries continue to pump out carbon dioxide, we should do our part. But that raises the most obvious question—and the one that Kyoto boosters have tried to quash whenever it is raised: What's so wrong with carbon dioxide anyway?

What's so wrong with carbon dioxide anyway? No one has ever died from atmospheric carbon dioxide poisoning. Which is good, considering it is a gas humans normally exhale.

No one has ever died from atmospheric carbon dioxide poisoning. Which is good, considering it is a gas humans normally exhale.

Carbon dioxide is required for plant life to grow—they consume it, and emit oxygen.

Carbon dioxide does not cause smog—that's the fault of ozone, particulate pollution, and sometimes other non-Kyoto gases including sulphur dioxide. Nitrous oxide (a minor Kyoto gas) can help cause ozone. But Canada's Environment Department notes that smog has traditionally

---

[77] Bjorn Lomborg, "The truth about the environment," *The Economist*, August 2, 2001.

been defined as "a mixture of smoke and fog."[78] The words "smoke," "fog" and "particles" are nowhere to be found in the Kyoto Protocol.

If you asked pollution-choked citizens of Mexico City or Calcutta or Soweto what environmental action they need most, cutting back on carbon dioxide wouldn't likely be on their top ten lists. Better sanitation, less smog, cleaner water, better health care would probably make their environmental "to do" list. Cutting back on carbon dioxide does none of these things.

If you asked pollution-choked citizens of Mexico City or Calcutta or Soweto what environmental action they need most, cutting back on carbon dioxide wouldn't likely be on their top ten lists.

LEVELS OF CARBON DIOXIDE ARE RELATIVELY LOW

A study in the prestigious scientific journal *Nature* shows that historically, carbon dioxide levels have often been higher—up to five times higher than they are today.[79] By studying the carbon dioxide content of various fossilized plants, scientists were able to estimate the carbon dioxide content in the air in prehistoric times. There was no fixed correlation between high carbon dioxide and global temperatures—in both ice ages and warm periods, carbon dioxide levels varied. But the one fact that the fossil studies showed was that carbon dioxide levels have historically been much higher than they are today.

---

[78] "Smog Fact Sheet," Environment Canada, Communications Directorate, August 23, 2002.

[79] Gregory J. Retallack, "A 300-million-year record of atmospheric carbon dioxide from fossil plant cuticles," *Nature* 411, May 17, 2001.

What would the Earth be like if carbon dioxide levels increased by 50 per cent—far higher than even the most pessimistic doomsday predictions? A team of scientists from North Carolina didn't guess, or dream up a computer program to reflect their own prejudices back at them. They actually went out into a forest, and set up a complex of pipes that, month in and month out, emitted carbon dioxide into the air. Within that circle, the carbon dioxide levels in the air were precisely 560 parts per million.[80]

The results? Not the death and destruction posited by the Kyoto boosters. Instead, the pine trees within the carbon dioxide bubble grew faster than those in the test sample, in regular 370 ppm air. Pine cones in the test sample had more seeds than regular pine cones. It was the true definition of the greenhouse effect: The trees were blooming more abundantly than before—hardly Maurice Strong's nightmare scenario of barren deserts and mass starvation.

By targeting carbon dioxide instead of real pollution, the Kyoto Protocol will have some perverse consequences. Take, for example, Regent Biologic Inc., a Canadian environmental clean-up company.

Regent uses naturally occurring bacteria to "eat" pollution—they have friendly bugs that detoxify everything from oil spills, to sewage overflows, without using chemicals to do it. The bacteria eat pollution—real, poisonous pollution—and emit harmless carbon dioxide. But under Kyoto, that carbon dioxide becomes the enemy, not the chemical spills themselves. "Even though the beneficial bacteria are naturally occurring and are not genetically engi-

---

[80] Laura Tangley, "High CO_2 Levels May Give Fast-Growing Trees an Edge," *Science*, vol. 292, April 6, 2001, p. 36.

neered or altered," says Robert Stokowski, Regent's president, "the interpretation of the Kyoto Protocol could significantly damage this emerging technology to deal with far greater contaminants in the environment than CO_2."[81]

As Stokowski points out, Kyoto won't stop bacteria that exist in nature from emitting carbon dioxide. But it will stop green businesses like his from putting those bacteria to work cleaning up real pollution.

Stokowski is all for pollution control—in fact, that's his business. But he thinks that any efforts to clean up the planet should be directed at environmental problems that genuinely hurt people—like the countless millions of citizens in Third World countries who do not have clean drinking water.

Bjorn Lomborg, a Danish environmentalist, stunned the pro-Kyoto community in 2001 with his blockbuster book[82] *The Skeptical Environmentalist.* Lomborg, the director of Denmark's Environmental Assessment Institute and a former Greenpeacenik, has better environmental credentials than most. His thesis is one that would probably get a better reception in the slums of Rio de Janeiro than at the UN conference there: If countries are going to spend money on the environment, they should fix real problems that affect real people today, not imaginary problems that might affect people a century from now.

Lomborg, who is also a professor of statistics at Denmark's University of Aarhus, points out that the projected cost of Kyoto for just one year—US $200-billion for

[81] Robert Stokowski, personal interview, November 6, 2002.

[82] Bjorn Lomborg, *The Skeptical Environmentalist*, Cambridge University Press, 2001.

the whole world—"could solve the single biggest problem in the world": dirty water in the Third World.[83] "This would save 2 million lives each year," he says, and "avert 500 million people getting seriously ill each year." What's more, says Lomborg, "this would just be the cost in 2010. We could do something equally good in 2011, 2012..."

> **For Lomborg, investing billions—trillions, over time—in Kyoto isn't just bad economics. It's bad environmentalism.**

Lomborg is no turbocapitalist. He doesn't work for Alberta's oilpatch. He's still a soft-hearted environmentalist, who really believes in saving the world. But, as a statistician, he has a hard head, too: He knows that, dollar for dollar, eliminating dirty drinking water will save millions more lives than eliminating clean carbon dioxide. Diverting money from a useful project to save lives to a pointless diplomatic treaty is "statistical murder." Lomborg wants to spend money cleaning up the world's problems. But he has the intellectual honesty to admit that "we need to prioritize correctly." For him, investing billions—trillions, over time—in Kyoto isn't just bad economics. It's bad environmentalism.

---

[83] Bjorn Lomborg, "The Real State of the World," speaking notes for The Fraser Institute lecture, Calgary, October 7, 2002.

CHAPTER EIGHT

The Truth About Global Warming

It should be obvious to anyone who has heard of the Earth's Ice Ages that our climate has changed before. Since we are no longer in an Ice Age, we know things have warmed up—and we are grateful for it. More importantly, from a Kyoto perspective, we know human-created greenhouse gases were not the cause of that historical warming. The last happy period of global warming was during the period of 850 AD to 1350 AD, a time-span dubbed the Little Climate Optimum or the Medieval Optimum. The Earth's atmosphere warmed by 2.5 degrees Celsius.

Rather than causing the catastrophes predicted by today's Kyotocrats:

> There were marked increases in agricultural productivity, trade, human amenities, and measurable improvements in human morbidity and mortality.[84]

It was during this period that the Vikings established a colony on Greenland—which, during this warm period, actually had green pastures on its southeastern coast. Grapevines flourished in southern England. No wonder

---

[84] Jerry Taylor, "Clouds Over Kyoto," *Regulation*, Winter 1998, p. 61.

climate historians call it the climate "Optimum." Of course, the human footprint on the environment was infinitely smaller than it is today, both as a function of the smaller medieval population, and the non-fossil fuel medieval economy. Simply put, humans didn't cause the Earth to warm; it happened naturally.

And it ended, naturally, too. What followed was called the "Little Ice Age," and the world saw "trade drop off, harvests fail, and morbidity and mortality rates jump largely due to an increase in diseases."[85] That Little Ice Age came to an end around 150 years ago, historically around the time of Confederation.

COMPUTER MODELING

How easy is it for scientists to predict the climate with precision? Anyone who watches the weather on the television news knows that predicting the temperature even one day into the future, in one city or town is a terribly inaccurate business—despite the use of high-tech satellites, computer models and experienced guesswork. If accurately predicting the local weather is challenging, how can climate scientists accurately predict the climate, for the entire world, for decades or even centuries in advance—with the absurd requirement of being precise to a tenth of a degree?

The answer, of course, is that such predictions are impossible. All climate projections are merely computer models, into which scientists try to take into account as many variables as they can, with whatever mathematical formulas they believe apply. More sophisticated models

---

[85] Taylor, p. 62.

take into account literally hundreds of factors—but, by necessity, contain thousands of best-guesses, or are simply silent on certain subjects. No one knows, for example, how to take into account the impact of solar flaring. Is it better to guess, or to leave that factor out? How can one predict spontaneous events, such as volcanoes, and their massive climactic impacts?

No model is better than the assumptions that went into its designing. By definition, models are nothing more than a collection of scientific theories, prejudices and guesses. As they say in computing, "garbage in, garbage out." Whatever is written into the models predetermines what they will predict about the future. That is the unhappy reason why, for example, new medicines must always be tested on animals, and then on human volunteers. A computer simulated prediction of how a new drug would work would, by definition, only take into account things we already know about biology, not things that we are about to learn. If we could make a computer model that would predict the outcome with certainty, we wouldn't need to use that model—we would already know how the drug would work.

Using computers to predict the future is simply a high-tech veneer over the plain fact that climate modeling is sheer guesswork.

Using computers to predict the future is simply a high-tech veneer over the plain fact that climate modeling is sheer guesswork.

As Dr. Gerald North, Distinguished Professor of Meteorology and Oceanography at Texas A&M University, argues, there are simply too many forces at play in nature to try to compute them all. According to Dr. North, even if scientists used the fastest computers available and took into account every possible variable, it would take a full month to run a point-by-point simulation of a single second's worth of weather changes, in a one kilometre cube. "One is forced to...the inevitable fudge-factors. We simply cannot get around it."[86]

Dr. Vincent Gray, one of the expert reviewers on the UN's IPCC climate science panel, points out that no UN climate model has ever successfully predicted any future climate sequence."[87] How could a model possibly predict the climate one year—or one hundred years—into the future, if it cannot predict tomorrow? Says Gray:

> Future forecasts presented by the IPCC are nothing but informed, but heavily biased guesses, processed by untested models. The forecasts are therefore easily manipulated to comply with current political expectations or demands.[88]

Like other climate scientists who criticize global warming orthodoxy, the UN probably won't seek his opinion again.

Terence Corcoran, the editor of the *Financial Post* and a long-time Kyoto skeptic, heaped scorn on scientists who put faith in untested models.

---

[86] Gerald North, *Climatic Change* (49:2001) as cited in "Science," June 27, 2001. On-line posting. Global Warming Information Page. <http://www.globalwarming.org>

[87] Vincent Gray, *The Greenhouse Delusion*, Multi-Science Publishing Co. Ltd., Essex, 2002, p. 2.

[88] Gray, p. 89.

Their output is all a product of their imaginations, possibly the greatest hypothetical modeling of human activity carried out by a government since Soviet bureaucrats tried to calculate how many shoes the Soviet Union would need over any five-year period.[89]

The trouble is, when models and reality clash, the UN often chooses to believe the model over what actually happens.

There are no carbon meters across the country. Instead, caged bureaucrats in Ottawa used Statscan numbers on energy use by sectors of the economy. They surveyed industries to ask them to estimate their carbon emissions, consulted experts, ran calculations through computers, guessed at this and that number, and ended up with gross estimates that look solid on paper. How much carbon do we produce driving to work, heating homes, running plants, mowing lawns, flying airplanes? Ottawa claims to know.

The flaws in modeling that Drs. North and Gray and others points out are to be expected. Models are guesses about reality; they can never be as accurate as reality itself. The trouble is, when models and reality clash, the UN often chooses to believe the model over what actually happens.

In the fall of 2002, for example, a study published in the journal *Geophysical Research Letters* [90] found that when scientists actually measured the temperature at the Earth's

---

[89] Terence Corcoran, "Make believe world of Kyotonomics," *National Post*, October 17, 2002.

[90] Chester Gardner et al, *Geophysical Research Letters,* August 28, 2002. On-line posting. Global Warming Information Page. <http://www.globalwarming.org>

North and South poles, it was dramatically colder than what the computer models predicted—22 to 28 degrees Celsius colder than the UN computers had guessed. The scientist who actually took the temperature remarked:

> In all fairness, since no one had made these measurements before, modellers have been forced to estimate the values. And, in this case, their estimates were wrong.

It's on the basis of jury-rigged models that Canada is hurtling towards economic hara-kiri. Now that many of those models are being disproved by actual scientific measurements, isn't it time Canada reconsider the Kyoto treaty?

THE EVIDENCE FROM SATELLITE RECORDS

Bold statements that the Earth has warmed up over the past century rely largely on thermometers scattered unevenly around the world, usually located in (warmer) population centers, such as cities. Since 1979, however, the National Oceanic and Atmospheric Administration has used orbiting satellites to measure the Earth's temperature with a high degree of accuracy—over all parts of the globe, from large cities to wide-open oceans or unpopulated jungles or forests. Analyzing these satellites' data is the specialty of Dr. John Christy, a "lead author" for the IPCC in 2001 and a PhD in Climate Dynamics. It's one of the main reasons he was chosen for the IPCC.

After 23 years of record-keeping,[91] Dr. Christy and his colleagues found that "since 1979, the global temperature trend is a modest +0.06 degrees Celsius increase per

---

[91] John Christy, "The Global Warming Fiasco," *Global Warming and Other Eco-Myths*, edited by Ronald Bailey, Competitive Enterprise Institute, 2002, p. 17.

decade"—or 160 years just to move one degree. At the same time, however, scientists using ground-based thermometers, located irregularly around the globe, "announced that the year 2001 was hot, the second warmest since records were first kept." The U.S. government satellite data for the same period, however, showed that 2001 was almost precisely "average" in terms of temperature.

"Unremarkable means unnewsworthy," writes Dr. Christy. "None of the wire services, to our knowledge, bothered to report this to the public." And when the IPCC conceded in its major 2001 report that it couldn't reconcile its earlier scattered, uneven, thermometer-based temperature readings with Dr. Christy's satellites,[92] that admission was ignored by the media, who had become fundamentalist Kyoto believers, with no room for heretical science.

The U.S. government data showed that 2001 was almost precisely average in terms of temperature.

Faced with Dr. Christy's impeccable data, the most common response by Kyoto boosters is to change the subject. In one debate in the *National Post,* Andrew Weaver, a Kyoto booster and climate scientist at the University of Victoria, was asked about Dr. Christy's data. Instead of rebutting 23 years of satellite readings, Dr. Weaver made a very unscientific appeal to emotion—and racial guilt. "I suggest this one be deferred to the Inuit people,"[93] he said. "There has been dramatic change."

---

92 "Summary for Policy-makers," *Third Assessment Report of Working Group 1,* Intergovernmental Panel on Climate Change, 2001, p. 9.

93 Andrew Weaver, "Kyoto: myths and science," *National Post,* November 14, 2002, p. A5.

Why would a PhD make such a bizarre rejection of space age science, in favour of stone age folklore? Would Dr. Weaver, who was recently awarded a $1.4-million, seven-year federal grant,[94] be in jeopardy of not having that grant renewed if he contradicted his political masters?

Dr. Christy is a dangerous man to the Kyoto Protocol for several reasons: His unimpeachable credentials mean that he must be taken seriously in the scientific community and by others who study the subject; his track record of actual scientific observation, using 23 years of real satellite data, makes his conclusions far more believable than others' best guesses and computer-generated predictions; and Dr. Christy has a very scientific habit of just plain asking questions.

Dr. Christy asks whether current climate predictions properly take into account the effect of clouds—some of which can increase the greenhouse effect, and some of which cool the Earth. He asks if predictions about the rising sea level properly take into account the recent and growing phenomenon of massive dams and man-made reservoirs, which keep water out of the sea. He points out that many of the IPCC's predictions are so minor that they are statistically irrelevant. For example, he says, the rate of sea level increase predicted by the IPCC is six inches per century—plus or minus four inches.[95] That's hardly alarming even if the worst case scenario were true. The fact that the UN scientists admit to a 66 per cent margin of error makes the

---

[94] Valerie Shore, "UVic climatologist wins national research fellowship," *The Ring*, March 7, 2002.

[95] John Christy, "The Global Warming Fiasco," *Global Warming and Other Eco-Myths*, edited by Ronald Bailey, Competitive Enterprise Institute, 2002, p. 22.

information nearly useless, and certainly not strong enough to destroy an economy over. If a political pollster made the same sort of statement—"40 per cent of Canadians support the Prime Minister, plus or minus 24 per cent"—everyone would know the information was useless. With sea level changes over the next century, it doesn't even matter whether it's two inches or ten: No one's basements are going to be flooded in Victoria or St. John's in the year 2100.

By what arrogance do the Kyoto boosters think they can predict with accuracy a century's worth of complex interactions involving the Sun, volcanic activity, the chlorophyll cycle of plants, winds, ocean currents, clouds and a thousand other factors, each alone more complex than we can predict?

Why should predicting the weather be any simpler or more accurate than predicting any other element of the biosphere? By what arrogance do the Kyoto boosters think they can predict with accuracy a century's worth of complex interactions involving the Sun, volcanic activity, the chlorophyll cycle of plants, winds, ocean currents, clouds and a thousand other factors, each alone more complex than we can predict? And if we cannot even predict the future, how do we summon the hubris to believe that we can change the future through Kyoto? Like King Canute, will we command the tides to stop?

THE NATURAL GLOBAL COOLING EFFECT

Over several days in June 1991, Mount Pinatubo in the Philippines erupted in a volcano. Millions of tonnes of gas and ash were spewed out in a matter of days—including gases that Kyoto seeks to limit, such as carbon dioxide, and other pollutants that Kyoto doesn't mention, such as sulphur dioxide. Pinatubo wasn't the largest volcano ever— not even the largest in the century. But, like Mount St. Helens before it, it allowed scientists to learn about what real emissions look like.

For example, nearly 20 million tonnes of sulphur dioxide was released from this one event.[96] By comparison, total sulphur dioxide emissions from Canada in 1999 were just 2.7 million tonnes. One week's emission from one volcano had as much ecological impact as all of Canada's cars and factories running at full bore, for seven years.[97]

But the massive emissions of gases from Mt. Pinatubo, including greenhouse gases such as carbon dioxide, didn't warm the Earth at all. In fact, according to the U.S. Geological Survey, all of those emissions actually

> caused global temperatures to drop temporarily (1991 through 1993) by about one degree Fahrenheit (0.5 degrees Celsius).[98]

Mt. Pinatubo wasn't the first time that global cooling set in because of volcanoes. In 1783, the Laki volcano in Iceland erupted, with the most emissions ever recorded in modern times. Benjamin Franklin, the U.S. scientist and diplomat, noticed the effect of this volcano a year later

---

96 U.S. Geological Survey, "The Cataclysmic 1991 Eruption of Mount Pinatubo, Philippines," Fact Sheet 113-97.

97 Canadian Environmental Protection Act, 1999—*CEPA Annual Report*, April 2000-March 2001, 2002, Department of Environment, Ottawa, p. 62.

98 U.S. Geological Survey, Fact Sheet 113-97.

during one of his many trips to Paris. Franklin himself theorized that the mass of volcanic gas and ash thrown into the atmosphere by a volcano could reduce the temperature on the surface of the earth. He wrote:

> During several of the summer months of the year 1783, when the effect of the sun's rays to heat the earth in these northern regions should have been greatest, there existed a constant fog over all Europe and a great part of North America...This fog was of a permanent nature; it was dry, and the rays of the sun seemed to have little effect towards dissipating it, as they easily do a moist fog arising from water.[99]

Franklin speculated about the source of the fog:

> The cause of this universal fog is not yet ascertained...the vast quantity of smoke, long continuing to issue during the summer from Hecla in Iceland, and that other volcano which arose from the sea near that island, which smoke might be spread by various winds over the northern part of the world, [the cause] is yet uncertain.

The massive Tambora volcanic eruption in Indonesia in 1815 brought about a "year without a summer," as it was called in North America. In New England, for example, "frost occurred during each of the summer months of 1816," according to the U.S. Geological Survey.[100]

---

[99] John Grattan, Lecture notes, "Climate in Britain and Europe and the Laki fissure eruption," The Institute of Geography & Earth Sciences, University of Wales, Aberystwyth.

[100] Richard S. Williams, Jr., *Glacier: Clues to Future Climate*, USGS General Interest Publication, 1999. On-line posting. U.S. Geological Survey. <www.usgs.gov>

So when Pinatubo blew its top in 1991, scientists—real scientists, not global warming scaremongers—knew what to expect. "The predicted and observed Pinatubo climatic cooling resulted in noticeable changes in the local climate and weather," wrote a team of scientists from the University of Hawaii. "For example, in 1992, the United States had its third coldest and third wettest summer in 77 years.[101] Funny—1992 was the year of the Rio Summit that whipped global warming into a pop-culture frenzy. A little detail such as 1992 being the coldest since the First World War didn't cause the UN a minute of self-doubt.

Volcanoes, of course, are not the solution to any real or imagined global warming. But the Earth's massive, natural volcanic history should be a lesson in humility to those who think that all changes in climate are caused by human activity— or the Kyoto premise, which is that human activity can stop climate changes. That is the classic definition of hubris. Maurice Strong, the Secretary-General of the Rio Earth Summit wrote in his eco-autobiography, "we are all gods now, gods in charge of our own destiny."[102] No doubt UN diplomats are some of the world's most powerful non-elected men. But not even they can do or undo in a lifetime what God or nature can do in a minute.

> **The Earth's massive natural volcanic history should be a lesson in humility for those who think that all changes in climate are caused by human activity.**

[101] Stephen Self et al., "The Atmospheric Impact of the 1991 Mount Pinatubo Eruption," *Fire and Mud*. On-line posting. U.S. Geological Survey. <http://pubs.usgs.gov/pinatubo/>

[102] Strong, p. 29.

CHAPTER NINE

The Media

Few media organs are as credible as mighty *Newsweek*, the U.S. magazine with a circulation of more than four million copies in 190 countries. Its readers are savvy—most have at least one university degree.[103] So when *Newsweek* warns about climate change, the world listens. After all, say the Kyoto boosters, who is more trustworthy—an eminent news magazine, with no particular agenda, or self-interested oil companies, who care less about pollution than about profits?

The magazine warned:

> There are ominous signs that the Earth's weather patterns have begun to change dramatically and that these changes may portend a drastic decline in food production—with serious political implications for just about every nation on Earth,

What's more:

> The evidence in support of these predictions has now begun to accumulate so massively that meteorologists are hard-pressed to keep up with it.

---

103 "Newsweek Circulation, Reader Profile and Advertising Rates," World Press Group, 2002.

To scientists, these seemingly disparate incidents represent the advance signs of fundamental changes in the world's weather. Meteorologists disagree about the cause and extent of the trend, as well as over its specific impact on local weather conditions. But they are almost unanimous in the view that the trend will reduce agricultural productivity for the rest of the century.

Newsweek knows what it would do, if only it were in charge:

The scientists see few signs that government leaders anywhere are even prepared to take the simple measures of stockpiling food or of introducing the variables of climatic uncertainty into economic projections of future food supplies. The longer the planners delay, the more difficult will they find it to cope with climatic change once the results become grim reality.

Climate change. Drought. Starvation. Panic-driven "solutions" such as stockpiling food. *There is no time to waste.*

The headline of this blockbuster *Newsweek* call to action? "The Cooling World"[104]—published on April 28, 1975.

Newsweek wasn't alone—a wave of global cooling panic swept the media.

Newsweek wasn't alone—a wave of global cooling panic swept the media. The story lost momentum in the late 1970s as the world found other things to fret about—the oil shocks and a world-wide recession. But the theme was

---

104 "The Cooling World," *Newsweek*, April 28, 1975, as reprinted in the *Financial Post*, June 21, 2000 p. C19.

picked up again with a vengeance in the late 1980s on the eve of the Rio Earth Summit—when global warming was christened the new threat.

On Earth Day 1970, the fashionable scientist was panicking about global cooling. "We have about five more years at the outside to do something," said Kenneth Watt, the 1970 equivalent to today's David Suzuki.

> If present trends continue, the world will be...11 degrees Celsius colder in 2000...about twice what it would take to put us into an ice age.

U Thant, then the Secretary-General of the UN, chimed in: Humanity had, at best, "perhaps 10 years left" before things would deteriorate out of control.[105] Ten years have gone by three times now; humanity is doing just fine, but U Thant and the global cooling fad are gone.

WHAT'S HAPPENING AT THE NORTH POLE?

The New York Times is not the world's largest newspaper or the oldest, but it is probably one of the most respected. And so when they ran a shocking story in August 2000 that the North Pole was melting, the world took notice. "The last time scientists can be certain that the Pole was awash in water was more than 50 million years ago,"[106] the *Times* concluded—proof positive that the globe was warming, and that humans probably had something to do with it. After all, this observation was made by no one

---

[105] Quoted in Tim Patterson and Tom Harris, "Profiting from panic," *Scripps Howard News Service*, April 5, 2001.

[106] *New York Times*, August 19, 2000, as cited in John Christy, "The Global Warming Fiasco," *Global Warming and Other Eco-Myths*, edited by Ronald Bailey, Competitive Enterprise Institute, 2002, p. 3.

less than James McCarthy, a Harvard professor who was on a polar cruise. Dr. McCarthy was also a senior United Nations' climate change expert. Does it get any more official than that?

But in the week that followed that breathless revelation, a number of people started to send the *Times* photographs they had taken, on trips to the North Pole years earlier, showing that melted slush and open water are not a new phenomenon at all. Eight days later, a blushing *Times* ran a correction. Reports of open water "are not as surprising as suggested."[107]

The embarrassing correction was buried in the paper but it did not escape the notice of late night comedian David Letterman. Two days later, he listed the "top ten signs the *New York Times* is slipping,"[108] including "instead of all the news that's fit to print, slogan [of the *Times*] is stuff we heard from a guy who says his friend heard about it" and "notice on sports page: all scores are approximate."

But some myths are just too juicy to be debunked. A year later, the *Times* heard "the seemingly indestructible snows of Kilimanjaro" were melting, and would be gone in the next 15 years."[109]

No messing around this time; the *Times* wrote a scorching editorial, directed to President George W. Bush, claiming this was

---

[107] *New York Times*, August 27, 2000, as cited in John Christy, "The Global Warming Fiasco," *Global Warming and Other Eco-Myths*, edited by Ronald Bailey, Competitive Enterprise Institute, 2002, p. 3.

[108] David Letterman, "Late Show Top Ten," CBS, August 30, 2000.

[109] "A global warning to Mr. Bush," *New York Times*, February 26, 2001.

further dramatic evidence of a relentless warming of the earth's atmosphere that cannot be explained by normal climate shifts and is at least partly traceable to the burning of fossil fuels like coal and oil.

Take that.

This time, it only took the *Times* three days to recant that global warming hysteria. The *Times* grudgingly published a letter pointing out that melting snow on Mt. Kilimanjaro had been happening for decades, and it "will continue to melt as long as the climate doesn't return to the temperatures of the Little Ice Age of past centuries." In fact, "weather satellites show a pronounced cooling trend of the atmosphere there."[110]

Why does the *New York Times*—whose motto is "all the news that's fit to print"—treat climate science as casually as it does? Why does a newspaper known for its intelligent treatment of other science news abandon its usual rigour for political polemics when global warming is the subject?

Perhaps it's because for the *Times*, and other liberal media, global warming has moved from the science pages onto the editorial and political pages—it is no longer an arcane subject of academic interest, but rather a subject loaded with political, economic and foreign affairs implications. Rigid standards of scientific truth have given way to malleable subjectivity once restricted to political and gossip columns. The editors of the *Times* gloss over the scientific doubt about global warming for the same reason they put global warming on their editorial pages in the first place: for the *Times*, and indeed most media, belief in global warming

---

[110] Fred Singer, "Mount Kilimanjaro is not a thermometer," *The New York Times*, March 1, 2001.

is a political statement about one's ideological identity. It's not about empirical measurements anymore.

Too bad. Because the world could use more dispassionate analysis of what is happening to our climate today.

BLAMING GLOBAL WARMING FOR THE WEATHER

Startling experiences, such as seeing water at the North Pole, or even watching tornadoes on television, can make it easy for normally skeptical consumers of media to believe that global warming is actually happening—even if the unusual weather isn't warm at all. Kyoto doomsayer Ross Gelbspan, who once wrote a book about global warming with such excited chapter titles as "The Coming Permanent State of Emergency,"[111] once published a letter to the *New York Times*, claiming "the most likely cause of the intense downpour on Thursday in New York was global climate change."[112] One day's rain—something that happens dozens of times each year in New York—is "most likely" because of global warming? This assessment by a reporter, not a scientist, was made based on watching the rain come down—no scientific investigation, just a hunch. But that is not the incredible part of the story—the incredible part is that the *New York Times* opinion page, possibly the most respected piece of real estate in journalism, actually felt this was news "fit to print."

Coincidentally, two Weather Channel meteorologists had a rebuttal to Gelbspan's hysteria in the next day's *USA Weekend*.[113] Weather has always been punctuated by

---

[111] Ross Gelbspan, *The Heat is On*, Perseus Publishing, 1997.

[112] Ross Gelbspan, *New York Times*, August 28, 1999.

[113] Colin Marquis and Stu Ostro, "Is the weather getting worse?" *USA Weekend*, August 29, 1999.

extreme events, argued Colin Marquis and Stu Ostro. But only the innovations of 24-hour news channels, the Internet and even 24-hour weather channels brought every unusual detail to the attention of anyone with a TV or a computer.

The two weathermen explained:

> Before, tornadoes ripped through Midwest towns, but consequences seemed more distant. Today, real-time multimedia communication means gripping images get beamed instantly from tornado alley into our living rooms…it's as if we're all experiencing the bad weather, albeit vicariously…

> As the population continues to grow, more people and buildings get in the way of whipping winds and flooding waters.

As well, the recent popularity of video cameras means that few tornadoes will go unfilmed—a limitation that would by definition keep such weather off of television. Marquis and Ostro call this:

> [The] X factor: storm chasers. Virtually non-existent in the '50s, there are now hundreds who tote palm-held camcorders into the Plains to tape the Big One.

"Is it getting hotter?" asked the two meteorologists. "Yes. But not as much as you'd think," they said—only half a degree Celsius over a century, relying on thermometers scattered unevenly across only certain inhabited parts of the world.

"Inevitably, talk of global warming increases during and just following extreme heat waves," they noted.

"Are there more hurricanes?" they asked. "No," they replied, pointing out that from 1940 to 1969, 23 hurricanes hit U.S. land; from 1970 to 1999, an equal time period, only 14 have. The only reason hurricanes seem more destructive, they point out, is that inflation and massive coastline development have put more people and property in the path of the few hurricanes that always have and always will blow ashore.

"Are there more tornadoes?" they ask. "Maybe," they say. "The number of *reported* tornadoes has more than doubled from the '50s to the '90s." But as Marquis and Ostro point out:

> If a tornado occurred and no one was around to see it or document its damage path, then for the purpose of official numbers, it truly did not occur. Even today, there is evidence suggesting that many tornadoes go undetected.

WHAT'S HAPPENING AT THE SOUTH POLE?

Like The *New York Times'* error about the North Pole, another popular urban legend is that the South Pole is melting, too. It is easy to see why this is a popular myth— it supports the myth that the sea level is rising and that Vancouver and Halifax will soon be underwater; and, being that no one lives in Antarctica, it's hard to debunk.

But a large team of Antarctic scientists did just that, in a stunning paper in *Nature* magazine, in January 2002.[114] Climate and environmental scientists from NASA, the U.S. Geological Survey and nearly a dozen universities checked to see if the computer models that Kyoto believers had been using were actually accurate. There's nothing like checking a

---

[114] Peter T. Doran et al., "Antarctic climate cooling and terrestrial ecosystem response," *Nature,* 415, January 31, 2002.

theory out in practice. Entitled "Antarctic climate cooling and terrestrial ecosystem response," the study shows that Antarctica has actually been cooling by 0.7 degrees Celsius per decade between 1986 and 2000—the period when the UN had claimed the Earth was at its hottest.

"Two or three years ago when we were waiting for the big summers, we noticed that they didn't come," said Dr. Peter Doran, the lead scientist in the study.[115]

For NASA and the other climate change scientists, the Antarctica study didn't match the computer modeling programs. The computers predicted that the Antarctic would warm up. Actually going to Antarctica showed that it was cooling down. Something had to give.

The UN and the Kyoto boosters decided to keep the computer models, and ignore the actual observations.

The UN and the Kyoto boosters decided to keep the computer models, and ignore the actual observations. As for Dr. Doran and his team, they acted like scientists ought to. They wrote:

Continental Antarctic cooling, especially the seasonality of cooling, poses challenges to models of climate, and ecosystem change.

The month before the UN meeting in Kyoto that drafted the Protocol, CBC's *The National* used Antarctica as part of a breathless sales pitch about the need for emergency action. Beginning an allegedly objective report on the subject, the show broadcast:

---

[115] *Washington Post*, January 14, 2002, as cited in "Science," January 23, 2002. On-line posting. Global Warming Information Page. <http://www.globalwarming.org>

Something ominous is happening at the bottom of the world. Parts of the continent of Antarctica are warming and melting.[116]

Given the debunking of the Antarctica myth, what's the likelihood of the CBC retracting that "ominous" prediction—or even not repeating it?

Nearly three months after the Antarctica error was corrected CBC's *The National* was at it again:

Another large piece of Antarctic ice has broken off and fallen into the sea. It's dramatic evidence that the climate is already changing, and it was reinforcement for Environment Minister David Anderson as he offered Ottawa's first ideas on how to cut Canada's greenhouse gas emissions.[117]

Who cares about accuracy? Icebergs mean drama—anyone who watched *Titanic* knows that. The CBC—a corporation wholly owned by the federal government, whose chairman is appointed by the Prime Minister—knows that Kyoto is a high priority. Accuracy is somewhere lower down the list.

CBC BIAS

The media bias in favour of Kyoto is palpable. The pro-Kyoto media seem to view Kyoto as a litmus test for environmentalism.

"Here's what that actually means," said Paul Hunter,[118] explaining Kyoto to a million viewers on CBC's *The National.*

---

[116] Eve Savory, *The National*, CBC, November 27, 1997.

[117] Kelly Crowe, *The National*, CBC, May 15, 2002.

[118] Paul Hunter, *The National,* CBC, September 3, 2002.

> By the year 2012, Canada will cut the amount of so-called greenhouse gases it produces, car exhaust for example, or smoke from coal-fired power plants, cut not by a little, but by a lot.

But Kyoto doesn't mention smoke at all. It doesn't mention soot, or dust or anything that most Canadians would normally consider to be pollution. Carbon dioxide is the number one gas Kyoto attacks. Methane—another naturally occurring gas—is the only other common gas regulated by the treaty. Nitrous oxide, or laughing gas and a host of very rare man-made gases round out the list.

Kyoto doesn't mention smoke at all. It doesn't mention soot, or dust or anything that most Canadians would normally consider to be pollution.

Or how about this lead-in to another Kyoto story, criticizing the U.S. for refusing to ratify Kyoto: "The cars we drive, the fuel we burn produces greenhouse gases—toxic gases that contribute to global warming."[119] It's debatable whether or not man-made greenhouse gases do contribute to global warming, or whether or not global warming actually exists. But no one, not even the most excitable Kyotocrat at the United Nations, would say that greenhouse gases from car emissions—water vapour and carbon dioxide—are toxic. That's the problem with calling carbon dioxide and other harmless emissions "pollution"—they don't fit into the neat journalistic preconceptions.

Even Alison Smith, the occasional anchor of CBC's *The National,* persists in claiming that Kyoto tackles real pol-

---

[119] Lynne Robson, *The National*, CBC, March 29, 2001.

lution. She once started a panel on the subject with "for more on the Kyoto developments and what they might mean for Canada's economy and smoggy skies..." Her guest, Jack Layton, then the president of the pro-Kyoto Federation of Canadian Municipalities, played right along—why should he shatter any helpful illusions? Canadians, he said, "are concerned about smog and about the future of the climate of the planet."[120] Of course they are. Because people such as Smith and Layton continue to mislead Canadians about what Kyoto actually cleans up.

CBC television, for example, broadcast a raft of critical stories when the government of Alberta launched a million-dollar ad campaign warning of Kyoto's economic costs. "It's a crime that a government can use the taxpayer's money to lie to the public," said one talking head, at the invitation of the CBC. No proof was offered that the Alberta ads were, indeed lies; and no Alberta politician or bureaucrat was given the opportunity to respond to the charge.[121]

The federal government's pro-Kyoto advertising campaign has been more or less ignored by the CBC, except for one feature prodding the feds for not propagandizing enough. "And what of the federal government's campaign to sell Kyoto?" asked *The National*.

> If indeed there even is one. There has been a newspaper ad campaign. And the Minister...often gives speeches about Kyoto.

And even that soft-soap treatment of the federal government's multi-million dollar Kyoto sales pitch can't resist

---

[120] Alison Smith, Jack Layton, *The National*, CBC, July 24, 2001

[121] John Bennett, *The National*, CBC, September 18, 2002.

calling the anti-Kyoto campaign by private business groups "propaganda"—a term not used for the federal minister's "speeches."[122]

When David Suzuki's environmental lobby group launched its pro-Kyoto campaign, the CBC was thrilled.

> An environmental think tank estimates Canadians could save $200 billion dollars if greenhouse gas emissions are cut in half by 2030.[123]

A week earlier, when the Canadian Chamber of Commerce had made the opposite announcement, the CBC took it upon itself to be the first line of defence for Kyoto purity. "It's the latest salvo in a propaganda war over the Kyoto Accord," said a broadcast describing itself somewhat liberally as "news." Unlike the Suzuki announcement, the CBC felt it necessary to rebut—or more accurately, to dismiss out of hand—the Chamber of Commerce campaign. "There were no solutions, no plan on offer, just more criticism of Ottawa," opined the CBC.[124] Another CBC reporter asked the Chamber's president, Nancy Hughes-Anthony, if the business community's request for a public debate was going to be the kind of consultation where the government sits down with business leaders, and the business leaders gripe, and gripe, and gripe?[125]

It is difficult to imagine this sort of hostile interrogation being directed towards a pro-Kyoto activist—especially ones, such as David Suzuki, who happen to be on the CBC payroll.

---

[122] Leslie MacKinnon, *The National*, CBC, October 22, 2002.

[123] Jill Dempsey, *CBC Radio*, October 2, 2002.

[124] Susan Murray, *CBC Radio*, September 26, 2002.

[125] Mary Lou Finlay, *CBC Radio*, September 26, 2002.

When it's not white-washing government spin, and labeling anti-Kyoto arguments "propaganda," the CBC engages in a little propaganda of its own. In one Kyoto special report, Peter Mansbridge asked:

> Where is the preponderance of scientific opinion on the basic scientific assumption of the Kyoto Protocol? What are we sure of?

Leslie MacKinnon, the reporter who answered, didn't miss a beat. She said:

> Scientists say there's just no doubt the weather is getting worse, and it's getting bad very quickly. The evidence is all around. Just this past weekend, Europe was battered by a storm of unusual and frightening violence.[126]

MacKinnon pointed out that there was a storm in Europe that was "frightening" and violent. That pretty much settles it.

"Scientists say," said MacKinnon—that's the CBC at its investigative best. And if the old "scientists say" routine still left some skeptics, MacKinnon pointed out that there was a storm in Europe that was "frightening" and violent. That pretty much settles it. Par for the course at the television network that once told Canadians "the flares in the Alberta oil fields have always cast an ominous glow"[127]—and called it a news report.

As Lee Morrison, a former MP and one of the most vocal critics of global warming hype, jokes:

---

[126] Peter Mansbridge, Leslie MacKinnon, *The National*, CBC, October 28, 2002.

[127] Kelly Crowe, *The National*, CBC, February 11, 1999.

Wilting in the heat? Blame greenhouse gases. A three-day killer blizzard in February? Clearly caused by excessive carbon dioxide emissions. Your husband is drinking, philandering and neglecting his personal hygiene? Unimpeachable evidence of global warming.[128]

A quick look at the UN's IPCC report in 2001 shows that it's doubtful MacKinnon actually checked to see what "the scientists" did say. Even the most pro-Kyoto element of the IPCC report—the media-friendly "summary for policy-makers," written by government bureaucrats, not climate scientists—found that there were no changes in storm "intensity and frequency" and "no significant trends evident over the 20th century."[129] MacKinnon thinks a "frightening" storm was because of global warming, but the UN scientists actually don't. They also put a lie to the media myth about other unusual weather events. "No systematic changes in the frequency of tornadoes, thunder days or hail events" were found either.

MacKinnon did mention that there are some "anti-Kyoto forces"—not scientists, or activists, or skeptics, but forces—who still resist the siren song of "scientists say" logic. MacKinnon said that the UN's IPCC scientists panel has "three times...confirmed the scientific basis of global warming," a significant finding. But the IPCC panel concluded no such thing. Its findings were that there was too much uncertainty to make a conclusion. It was only the political summary of the IPCC science—cre-

---

128 Lee Morrison, "Has Alberta fallen victim to Kyoto fever?," *Calgary Herald*, November 9, 2002, p. OS7.

129 "Summary for Policy-makers," *Third Assessment Report of Working Group 1*, Intergovernmental Panel on Climate Change, 2001, p. 5.

atively edited at UN headquarters—that gave global warming any basis, but nowhere in it did the scientists engage in violent weather fear-mongering, or blame particular incidents on global warming. MacKinnon just made that up herself.

Mansbridge then asked another CBC reporter, Bob McDonald, what he thought about the science behind Kyoto. "The sad thing about that," answered McDonald, the host of CBC radio's *Quirks and Quarks,* "is that science by its nature has uncertainties." Most scientists might not look at uncertainty with sadness; but for Kyoto advocates such as McDonald, action is more important that accuracy. "The problem," said McDonald, is that if the media listens to those voices of uncertainty, "you're talking to the extremists, they're the minority." It's not often that scientists refer to each other as extremists; but McDonald isn't a scientist himself. He's a CBC journalist on a mission. "Everyone is saying look, we do need to do something about this. The science is really solid," he added. At the CBC, like many other activist media, the truth about global warming is decided by a show of hands, not by empirical studies by "extremists."

At the CBC, like many other activist media, the truth about global warming is decided by a show of hands, not by empirical studies by "extremists."

Or, said McDonald, they're unqualified.

> The skeptics who go against it, yeah, medical doctors, geologists, people in other professions were not climate scientists and their arguments when you look at them closely just don't stand up.

This is what McDonald concluded, himself a journalist who specializes in programming for kids. His view—the CBC view—is simple. If you support Kyoto, you are credible— and no matter what your credentials, you are an extremist if you don't agree. But, in fact, the vast majority of experts that McDonald claims support the Kyoto theory aren't climate experts either. In fact, there are only about 60 PhD's in climatology in the entire United States,[130] and far fewer in Canada. McDonald has yet to denounce David Suzuki's Kyoto opinions, even though he is a geneticist.

If you support Kyoto, you are credible—and no matter what your credentials, you are an extremist if you don't agree.

So how did McDonald, the CBC's impartial arbiter of science end his exposition? With a call to political action, of course. "We can afford to do it," he said. "So we should." Ah. The scientific method in action. No wonder McDonald's science show has been dubbed *Quirks and Quacks* by Kyoto skeptics.[131]

CITY-TV

The CBC isn't alone in its pro-Kyoto propaganda. Like David Suzuki on CBC, Toronto's CITY-TV station also has a self-described Kyoto activist on their payroll. Bob Hunter, a Canadian co-founder of Greenpeace, and a "reporter" for CITY-TV in Toronto, doesn't just "report" the news on

---

[130] Patrick J. Michaels, "Holes in the Greenhouse Effect?" *The Washington Post*, June 30, 1997.

[131] Terence Corcoran, "Quirks and Quacks," *National Post*, November 5, 2002, p. F15.

Kyoto, he makes the news. In November 2002, Hunter called Alberta Premier Ralph Klein and Ontario Premier Ernie Eves "ecological criminals"[132] for opposing Kyoto, and claimed that a public opinion survey that showed opposition to Kyoto growing, "was, in fact, fraudulent." When Ipsos-Reid, the internationally-respected pollster that conducted the poll threatened to sue, Hunter issued a grovelling apology, admitting that the poll indeed "impartially and accurately" measured the mood of the country, and that his statements were "without foundation."[133] Klein and Eves did not threaten to sue over Hunter's allegation that they have committed crimes, so he has yet to retract that inflammatory statement. None of which seems to perturb the management at CITY-TV.

It wouldn't be accurate to call most journalists covering the Kyoto beat "reporters." They're editorialists, dressing up their ideological views as news and censoring or ridiculing any skeptics who dare defy political correctness.

---

[132] Gloria Galloway, "Kyoto backer lambastes Klein, Eves," *The Globe and Mail*, November 6, 2002 p. A5.

[133] "Activist and CITY-TV Commentator, Bob Hunter, Issues Full Retraction and Apology to Ipsos-Reid for Remarks Made on Kyoto Poll," Press release, Ipsos-Reid, November 8, 2002.

CHAPTER TEN

The Kyoto Kamikazes

What motivates Kyoto's supporters? Why are they so passionate, even extreme?

For a few Svengalis such as Maurice Strong, the UN's senior environmental bureaucrat, it is the thrill of writing a planet-wide law establishing a new economic and environmental order. Kyoto inches us closer to a world where countries and nations cease to act as political forces. They are replaced by global bureaucrats, with law-making and law-enforcement powers.

For some ideologues, such as the union bosses at the Canadian Labour Congress, Kyoto is an attack on international corporations—so by definition, it is welcomed by class warriors. Rank and file union members at steel mills, auto plants and oil refineries might have a different view of Kyoto, but they don't get to spend the union dues budget on lobbyists.

For some, Kyoto is a Trojan Horse, a stealthy way to make wealthy countries pay tens of billions of dollars in foreign aid each year. By establishing unrealistic emissions reduction targets, the Kyoto Protocol guarantees that countries that ratify will be forced to invest in development projects in Third World countries, or just pay straight cash for imaginary emissions permits.

For most Canadians, Kyoto is an idealistic expression of environmental responsibility. Virtually no one in Canada has read the actual Protocol, and so each Canadian can project onto Kyoto whatever comfortable environmental aspirations they might have—from cutting back on smog (which is not covered by Kyoto's list of gases) to saving the world from global warming (the UN science panel says Kyoto will only delay, not stop any possible warming).

Until Kyoto is actually implemented, it means nothing to Canadians other than an abstract discussion on the news each night, or a telephone call from a public opinion pollster. No wonder David Anderson, the Environment Minister wants to vote on Kyoto before telling Canadians how it will be achieved. "The ratification issue is separate from the development of a plan,"[134] he says.

But there are some people who support Kyoto for another reason altogether: Because it controls people.

Kyoto tells big businesses what they can and can't do— that's why Canada's left-wing union bosses love it. But it also tells ordinary Canadians what they can and can't do.

To make a 30 per cent reduction in emissions will mean that each Canadian must reduce our use of energy by 30 per cent, on average—the "lifestyle shifts" called for by Anderson's economists.[135] Less driving. More buses. Less heat in the winter, less air conditioning in the summer. Parking lot taxes. SUV taxes. Less air travel. Even colder showers.

Kyoto appeals to activists who want to control others, because they have been unable to shape public opinion and

---

[134] David Anderson, press conference at the Halifax Environment and Natural Resources Ministers meeting, October 29, 2002.

[135] Mark Jaccard, "Costing Greenhouse Gas Abatement," *Isuma*, Winter 2001.

change public behaviour voluntarily, through persuasion. As Lorne Gunter, a leading Kyoto critic, sees it:

> These eat-your-peas busybodies are delighted by any opportunity that presents itself to tell us how to live our lives more correctly.[136]

Kyoto will order by law what these interventionists have been unable to achieve through appeals to reason.

PROFESSIONAL ENVIRONMENTAL ADVOCATES

David Suzuki is one such Kyoto fanatic. Perhaps that's why he promotes it with the rhetoric of a preacher, not the logic of a scientist. He told a news conference:

> I want to remind you that before the civil war in the U.S., the southern states said, "We can't afford to abolish slavery. It'll ruin our economy." Some things have to be done just because they're right.[137]

That's not the language of methodical scientific observation and analysis. That's the language of radical politics, of personal insults and aspersions. It's the language of control.

Suzuki has railed on about the environment for years, always hyping the next fashionable calamity or crisis, often at taxpayers' expense. Like David Anderson, Suzuki is used to total unanimity—he surrounds himself with fellow Kyoto travellers—and can lose his temper when challenged. At one global warming town hall meeting in 1999, a lone Kyoto skeptic dared to politely question Suzuki about the science.[138] Jumping into action, the town hall's moderator repeatedly turned off the skeptic's microphone, with

---

136 Lorne Gunter, personal interview, November 12, 2002.

137 David Suzuki, *CTV News*, September 25, 2002.

Suzuki's beaming approval. How dare some lowly citizen question him, Canada's leading scientific celebrity!

Canadians find him entertaining, but so far haven't modeled their lives on his New Age aphorisms. "I've been a total failure,"[139] he told the *Montreal Gazette* in November 2002. Of course Suzuki hasn't been a failure: He has had a fabulously successful career as an entertainer on television and radio, and his lobby group fundraises at an enormous clip. But, despite forty years of earnest, sometimes self-righteous propagandizing, Canadians just haven't followed his political admonitions. SUVs are as popular as ever. Nobody wants to take the bus in the middle of a Canadian winter.

That, he says, is his failure. His true mission of social activism has failed.

But what do frustrated politicians do when the public rejects them, again and again? Perhaps they abandon their belief in the wisdom of the people, and in democracy itself. If, after decades of cajoling, Canadians won't voluntarily adopt Suzuki's views, then Kyoto is just the antidote—it will force them to live by Suzuki's laws, even if they don't agree.

For Ron de Burger of the Canadian Public Health Association, it's about control, too. Doctors can tell only their own patients what to do; for de Burger and his busybodies, Kyoto makes 31 million Canadians subject to their doctors' orders. He said:

---

138 Laurie Lemoine, "Suzuki brooks no critics," *The Ottawa Citizen*, April 1, 1999.

139 Jeff Heinrich, "Suzuki says he's failed in mission," *Montreal Gazette*, November 9, 2002.

Ratifying the Kyoto Protocol is a powerful step to start reducing fossil fuel use, which means improved air quality and public health.[140]

The Toronto Star was thrilled—it carried the story prominently, with a headline that screamed "Kyoto: It's a life saver, MDs say," claiming that:

Implementing the accord could prevent 6,000 people in Ontario...from dying prematurely each year as a result of smog-related illness.[141]

No doubt de Burger meant well—he wants to control peoples' activity, because he knows better than they do. He and the other doctors and health bureaucrats who endorsed Kyoto that day probably do think that Kyoto cracks down on smog—smog that may well kill thousands of people a year. Trouble is, Kyoto doesn't mention smog at all. Canada could double our smog output, and still be within Kyoto's rules. Kyoto cuts down on carbon dioxide—and surely even the most politicized doctor wouldn't claim the gas that we naturally exhale is killing thousands of Canadians each year.

Suzuki has gone far beyond being an objective scientist. He is now a full-time agitator, with his own lobby group, modestly named the David Suzuki Foundation, and supported by taxpayers through its federal charitable tax status—and through the CBC. In 2002, Suzuki's vanity foundation published a study called *The Bottom Line on Kyoto*, claiming that cutting Canada's carbon dioxide emissions by

---

[140] Ron de Burger, *CTV Newsnet*, September 25, 2002.

[141] Les Whittington, "Kyoto It's a life saver, MDs say," *The Toronto Star*, September 26, 2002, p. A6.

more than 100 megatonnes—roughly half the Kyoto requirements—would actually create jobs and grow the economy. Suzuki is a geneticist by training, but that didn't stop him from trying his hand at politics and economics.

Suzuki argued that by forcing families and factories to be more energy efficient, Canada would save money under Kyoto. But as Ross McKitrick, an economist at the University of Guelph points out:[142]

> If there really are spectacular business opportunities out there that reduce emissions while paying millions of dollars in new net earnings...all those profit-hungry corporations will get the job done just fine on their own.

McKitrick's point is so obvious that it often gets overlooked: If it was economically sensible for companies to cut back on their energy use, they would do it on their own. But massive energy reductions are either impossible (as in the steel and auto industries) or would have to be made up through other, costly substitutes. If Kyoto really is a magical economic fountain of youth for Canada, one has to wonder why only David Suzuki, an environmental fundamentalist, has seen it and Canada's profit-oriented businesses and investors haven't. Says McKitrick:

> You can't claim that Kyoto is a financial bonanza and at the same time claim it is so costly firms need to be forced into compliance.

---

[142] Ross McKitrick, *Financial Post*, October 19, 2002 p. FP11.

But even the fine print in Suzuki's own study shows that he fudged the data to make the economics look good.

> No one has claimed that Kyoto will reverse global warming. It is a modest first step. By expert estimates, humanity must reduce emissions by 60 or 80 per cent to stabilize the climate.[143]

Suzuki's dubious study looked at the economic consequences of reaching only half of Kyoto's targets, or about 15 per cent in reductions. But in the same document, Suzuki himself warns that cuts up to five times deeper will have to be made, to satisfy him and his lobby group.

To make his fantasy numbers work, Suzuki had to include some real whoppers into his calculations. For example, his study assumed that tens of thousands of Canadian workers would simply not go to work anymore—they would be forced to work from home, instead of going into the office, in "mandatory" programs affecting any business with more than 50 employees. Hundreds of thousands more would be forced to carpool, or not be allowed to drive—again, through "mandatory," police-enforced laws. And free parking in Canada would be outlawed—a $2 global warming parking tax would tack on to every car ride.

To be fair, many of these invasive schemes weren't dreamed up by Suzuki, but by federal bureaucrats, desperate to find a way to get people out of cars. [144]

---

143 Tellus Institute and MRG & Associates, *The Bottom Line on Kyoto*, April 2002.

144 "A Discussion Paper on Canada's Contribution to Addressing Climate Change," Government of Canada, Ottawa, 2002, p. 51, and Tellus Institute and MRG & Associates, *The Bottom Line on Kyoto*, April 2002.

Ipsos-Reid, one of Canada's blue-ribbon pollsters, decided to test the popularity of a few Kyoto schemes. In one provincial survey,[145] they asked whether or not people would be willing to lower the temperature in their hot-water tank at home. Eighty seven per cent of respondents said they would—if, indeed, it would save the planet. (The survey was taken in the daytime and evening in the month of May; perhaps respondents' exuberance about taking cool showers would have been more restrained had the question been asked of them on a cold December morning.)

But taking cold showers won't make much of a dent in Canada's emissions at all—certainly not the 30 per cent required by Kyoto. In the words of Mark Jaccard, a federal government Kyoto expert, only "high price shocks"[146] will get Canadians to lay off of carbon-based fuels. Turning down the hot water is one thing; but when Ipsos-Reid tested the public's appetite for higher energy prices, support plummeted. Only 11 per cent of respondents said they would be "very willing" to pay more for gas at the pump, or for household energy costs. It's hard to imagine that Canadians in any province would embrace yet another gasoline price hike.

Only 11 per cent of respondents said they would be "very willing" to pay more for gas at the pump, or for household energy costs.

That's not the only fact-bending used to make the numbers in *The Bottom Line on Kyoto* work out. Suzuki states that "Canada is hesitating while Japan,

---

[145] Ipsos-Reid, *Albertans and the Kyoto Protocol*, May, 2002.

[146] Mark Jaccard, "Costing Greenhouse Gas Abatement," *Isuma*, Winter 2001.

Russia...and many others are in the final stages of ratification." That may be theoretically true—Japan formally ratified the treaty in June 2004—but that country has not yet put it "into force"—its economy is just too frail to absorb that unnecessary punishment. Other than express Japan's abstract support for reducing greenhouse gases, and engaging in a P.R. campaign, Japan's implementation law is non-existent.[147] And although Suzuki is technically accurate, when he states that Russia will sign, it is misleading in the extreme not to disclose that Russia does not have to reduce its emissions of carbon dioxide by one breath under Kyoto.

THE FEDERATION OF CANADIAN MUNICIPALITIES

At the end of the day, Suzuki has no power other than the power of propaganda. A greater danger lies with government-funded pro-Kyoto lobby groups. Like Suzuki, they give the impression of a chorus calling for Kyoto, when really it is just an act of ventriloquism—the federal government and the UN funding activists to tell them what they want to hear.

By far the largest pro-Kyoto lobby funded by Canadian taxpayers is the Federation of Canadian Municipalities. Essentially a club for Canada's mayors and aldermen, the FCM was turned into Canada's largest pro-Kyoto campaign organization through a $250-million grant from Paul Martin—Maurice Strong's protégé.

Martin wrote a gushing blurb for Strong's radical environmentalist autobiography, calling Strong's ideas "a well-

---

[147] "Kyoto Pact legislation being prepared for Diet," *The Japan Times*, February 18, 2002.

elaborated plan for much needed reform."[148] More important than that praise for an old friend is Martin's $250-million environmental grant to the Federation of Canadian Municipalities, one of the last big spending items that Martin pushed through as Finance Minister.[149] That quarter-billion dollar slush fund is earmarked for cities, but only if they sign onto the Strong-Martin environmental agenda. As Martin told the House of Commons when he unveiled his 2000 Budget, he had "launched the process required to develop a national climate change strategy" and that climate change was an "unequivocal fact." Canada's municipal politicians, ever-eager for more funds, happily signed on to Martin's "strategy"—and a hundred Canadian city and town councils have been acting as lobbyists for Kyoto ever since.

This year, the FCM selected a new president—John Schmal, an alderman from Calgary. Schmal has toned down the rabid Kyoto rhetoric of his predecessor, New Democrat Jack Layton. The Government of Alberta has even put out a press release claiming that Schmal is in favour of Premier Klein's go-slow plan on emissions reductions. Perhaps he is. But the FCM itself is ignoring its new president—a quick glance at its website[150] shows that its Kyoto campaign is still in high gear. Page after page exhorts Canadians to "Help make a difference by supporting ratification of the Kyoto Protocol." Perhaps Schmal might want to take a trip to Toronto to acquaint himself with the organization he allegedly leads.

---

[148] Strong, back cover.

[149] Department of Finance, *Budget 2000*, February 28, 2000.

[150] On-line posting. Federation of Canadian Municipalities. <http://www.fcm.ca>

He will find the quarter-billion dollar Kyoto slush fund remains. And the FCM's director of environmental policy, Louise Comeau, is still in charge. As a former campaign director for the radical Friends of the Earth lobby group and the Sierra Club, she remains the power behind the throne at FCM. While Schmal spends his time tending to constituents in his Calgary ward, Comeau continues her Kyoto campaign unsupervised, thousands of kilometres away from her Calgary boss. According to Elizabeth May, the current Executive Director of the Sierra Club, Comeau "is the most influential climate activist in Canada."[151] She gushed:

Louise Comeau, the former campaign director for the radical Friends of the Earth lobby group and the Sierra Club remains the power behind the throne at the FMC.

If you ask anyone in government or industry who is behind the pressure on government to deal with climate change, they'd just say Louise—they wouldn't even use her last name.

One would think that Canadian cities and towns have more pressing issues than reducing carbon dioxide—a matter that is constitutionally shared between provincial governments and the federal government, leaving no jurisdiction for cities. And even where cities do have environmental concerns—reducing smog, for example—Kyoto does nothing towards that end. Smog is not carbon dioxide, or methane, or the other, rarer Kyoto greenhouse gases. It is

---

151 Judi McLeod, "Federation of Canadian Municipalities Hijacked by Left," *Toronto Free Press*, May 10- June 2, 2001.

an airborne mixture of particulate pollution, sulphur and other chemicals, none of which Kyoto tackles. In most civic elections, however, climate change just isn't a campaign issue—taxes are, or rejuvenating run-down neighbourhoods. Nonetheless, in its official policy development book, the Federation of Canadian Municipalities says it:

> will urge municipal governments, through their own operations and policies, to support the principles and agreements adopted at the 1992 Earth Summit, as well as the framework Convention on Climate Change, the 1997 Kyoto Protocol and the Biodiversity Convention.[152]

Climate change is an artificial agenda, bought and paid for by Paul Martin, using federal taxpayers' money, in the service of the federal Liberal party's agenda—and the UN's, too. Municipal voters across Canada had no say in the adoption of this Kyoto manifesto. Then again, voters around the world had no say in the adoption of the Kyoto Protocol in the first place.

POLITICIANS PLAYING TO PUBLIC OPINION

Kyoto has been such a public relations success that politicians and other Kyoto boosters feel no shyness about jumping on the science bandwagon with incredible scientific allegations of their own. Tim Sale, Manitoba's Energy Minister, charmed an Ottawa press conference by talking about cuddly polar bear cubs. As the press gallery cooed on demand, Sale claimed:

> We've got our cute polar bears that are unfortunately getting thinner because they're not staying on the ice long

---

[152] McLeod, 2001.

enough and they're not bearing cubs that live as long or as often...That's a consequence of the fact that the ice pack is melting sooner.[153]

Sale is not a climatologist—he is a former business consultant and church minister. But that didn't matter. He had pictures of cute polar bears.

Everyone's getting in on the game. David Anderson, the Environment Minister, told Parliament that:

> The North...is the area which perhaps is experiencing the most severe impacts of climate change. We see that the ice is melting. Polar bears are starving. The traditional lifestyle of Aboriginal peoples is threatened. The fauna and flora are highly disturbed.[154]

The history of Parliament has rarely seen a more alarmist generalization. That the minister felt comfortable making that statement without citing any supporting studies only confirms the blind faith upon which his colleagues have accepted the rationale for Kyoto. Throw in a pinch of liberal guilt about Aboriginal assimilation, and Anderson's speech was the perfect politically correct cliché.

Paul Okalik, the Premier of Canada's Nunavut Territory, says he knows that man-made carbon dioxide emissions are causing the atmosphere to warm. After all, he told fawning reporters:

> I decided to bring [my children] along and to cross the river that we used to cross when I was their age. It hadn't

---

[153] David Gamble, "Minister touts Kyoto as polar bears' cure," *Calgary Sun*, October 26, 2002.

[154] David Anderson, *Hansard*, February 2, 2001.

rained for over a month and we couldn't cross that river. You know why?

The Premier, a lawyer by training, not a scientist, asked the media. The press gallery leaned forward, delighted by this anecdote, by far more compelling than some stuffy scientific paper on the subject. "The glaciers were melting. And we couldn't even cross those rivers anymore."[155]

It was a moving story, of course—which mattered far more than the fact that it was utterly false. As Lorne Gunter points out:[156]

> Between 1814 and 1817, [the Arctic] warmed so much for so long that English explorers and merchants dared hope a prosperous new era was commencing. The Royal Society deduced "a considerable change of climate...must have taken place in the Circumpolar Regions, by which the severity of the cold that has for centuries past enclosed the seas in the high northern latitudes in an impenetrable barrier of ice has...greatly abated.

One hundred fifty years before 38-year old Premier Okalik was gallivanting about the creeks of Nunavut, scientists of the day noted the global warming. Unlike Premier Okalik, they didn't have the political savvy to ascribe that warming to the steel industry or the teeming masses of SUVs, because those scapegoats for natural climate fluctuation were still a century away.

---

[155] Paul Okalik, *CBC Radio*, August 2, 2002.

[156] Lorne Gunter, "Canadian Hot Spots," *Tech Central Station*, September 27, 2002.

CHAPTER ELEVEN

A Made in Canada Recession

So Jean Chrétien got what he wanted: Canada "beat" the U.S. by signing on to deeper cutbacks in energy use under Kyoto. Canadian families are now about to find out what it feels like to turn the economic clock back twenty years.

A study published in the Winter 2001 edition of Canadian government policy magazine called *Isuma*, has a startling prediction—all the more, considering it was paid for by the pro-Kyoto Liberal government. Mark Jaccard and a team of ten researchers in the School of Environmental Management at Simon Fraser University used a painstakingly meticulous series of calculations to find out just how much it would cost to gut our economy to Kyoto levels.[157]

Forty-five-billion dollars was their answer. "This is equivalent to a one-year recession," Jaccard wrote.

What if Canada is already in a recession—or trying hard to stay out of one, as we are now? Right now—pre-Kyoto—Canada's economy is just sputtering along, not quite meeting an economist's technical definition of a recession, but not exactly booming, either.

---

[157] Mark Jaccard, "Costing Greenhouse Gas Abatement," *Isuma*, Winter 2001.

Our unemployment rate, for example, has been slowly ratcheting up for more than two years, from a low of just over six per cent in 2000, to close to eight per cent in recent months. Now a government publication forecasts a one-year, made-in-Kyoto recession. Great.

But a one-year recession isn't the worst of it. Jaccard and his team calculated that the only way to cut energy use by Canadians enough to please the Kyoto bureaucrats, is for massive "lifestyle shifts." And the only way to force Canadians into lifestyle shifts is through "high price shocks"—such as jacking up the price of gasoline to $1.10 per litre. Or doubling household power bills. And increasing the cost of gas by 60 per cent.

What kind of government would willingly do that to its own citizens—would willingly cut families' pay-cheques, force businesses to lay off employees and cancel expansion plans? What kind of country volunteers for a man-made recession? Who could recommend an energy policy that includes $1.10 per litre for gasoline? And all of this in the name of an global environmental theory that is shaky at best, and utterly unachievable even on its own shaky scientific terms without the participation of the rest of the world?

THE ANALYSIS AND MODELING GROUP

Incredible as it may sound, Jaccard's depressing study was the federal government's attempt to put a happier face on the results of their earlier study on the economic impact of Kyoto. After Kyoto was signed in December 1997, the federal government, along with the provinces and terri-tories, decided to study the economic impact of reducing emissions. That in itself is a scandal—that Canada would *first* sign a treaty requiring us to make massive personal and industrial changes, and *then* do a study to see what the cost would be.

In April 1998, the federal, provincial and territorial Ministers of Energy and Environment formed the National Climate Change Process to do these economic studies. One of the groups set up by this process was called the Analysis and Modeling Group (AMG), which, as its name would suggest, was in charge of fiddling around with economic numbers to see if it was possible to meet Kyoto targets—and if so, how much it would cost.[158]

When AMG published its 100-page study in November 2000 it would have caused an uproar, if the Canadian media or industry leaders had been following the Kyoto debates.

AMG took its time to do a thorough job—there were more than a dozen watchful eyes on the committee, representing everyone from Ontario's Ministry of Finance to the Newfoundland and Labrador Department of Mines and Energy. Five experts from the federal government were on the panel too. When AMG published its 100-page study in November 2000 it would have caused an uproar, if the Canadian media or industry leaders had been following the Kyoto debates in any serious way. Back then, however, the report was just another eye-glazing bundle of computer models, estimates and predictions about a treaty that most Canadians had never heard about.

---

[158] Analysis and Modeling Group, National Climate Change Process, *An Assessment of the Economic and Environmental Implications for Canada of the Kyoto Protocol,* November 2000, p. 88.

Reading the report today, on the eve of the Kyoto Protocol being made into Canadian law, the AMG report is a shocking warning. Nearly every single page is packed with economic bad news—and this from a research committee stacked with experts appointed by the pro-Kyoto federal government.

Reaching Kyoto targets would mean "sustained, long-term negative economic impacts," wrote AMG.[159] By the time Kyoto fully kicks in, in 2010, a typical Canadian family of four would be $4,400 poorer a year, every year—or $40-billion a year for the whole country.[160] That's because Canadians would face "higher production costs, deterioration in competitiveness and lower incomes"—an "adjustment period" that the government says "is expected to be lengthy, perhaps as long as 15 years."[161] And, contrary to conventional wisdom, the hardest-hit province would not be Alberta, but Ontario and Saskatchewan.

Don't bother complaining to David Anderson, the Environment Minister, about that. He'll call you selfish and greedy—and say you would probably waste the money anyway. He said:

> I just can't think of any Canadian that I've talked to who says I don't care what happens to my great-grand-children, I just want to have an extra $200 a year or $500 a year to spend on drink and cigarettes.[162]

---

[159] AMG, p. 89.

[160] AMG, p. xiv.

[161] AMG, p. 49.

[162] David Anderson, *CBC Radio*, May 18, 2002.

That's easy to say for an independently wealthy cabinet minister with a six-figure salary and a gold-plated pension. For most Canadian families, however, losing a month's pay each year will cut into a lot more than just "drink and cigarettes."

The AMG study tested different computer models with different "assumptions." For example, it estimated the economic impact on Canada in three different Kyoto scenarios: If the United States takes an aggressive approach to meet its Kyoto emissions reductions, by buying billions of dollars in "emissions credits" from developing countries; if the U.S. aggressively lowered its own emissions; or if Canada essentially implemented Kyoto alone. The first two possibilities were Canada's best-case economic scenarios; any calculations done in economic models where the U.S. did not participate demonstrated much more pronounced damage to Canada's economy. The computer models in that case confirmed what makes sense intuitively: If Canada slaps massive new taxes, regulations and restrictions on our economy, but our major trading partner and competitor does not, we will fall even further behind, economically.

The authors of the AMG study cling to the hope that the U.S. would engage in a massive Kyoto program, involving huge purchases of "emissions credits." After all, they wrote in November 2000, that approach "approximates the Clinton Administration's preferred position."[163]

But by November 2000, Bill Clinton's final term was over. And even if Al Gore had won the Florida recount and beat George W. Bush in the month after the AMG report was released, it would not have changed the fact

[163] AMG, p. 19.

that the U.S. Senate voted unanimously against Kyoto—and specifically against the type of international emissions credit shell game that AMG was counting on for their rosy predictions.

For Canada, the hard math of Kyoto comes down to this: if current trends continue, Canada will emit 809,000,000 tonnes (809 megatonnes) of carbon dioxide by the year 2010. Canada's Kyoto target, however, is 571 megatonnes—or about 240 megatonnes less. Even if Canada can get credit for our forests and other plants, the gap is still 216 megatonnes.[164] AMG estimates that the cost of reducing each tonne could be up to $120 on average[165]—and nearly three times that for small industry and the transportation sector.[166] The oil and gas "upstream and refining sector"—the business of finding crude oil and turning it into gasoline "had insufficient measures to meet its emission target," no matter what the price. For the oil and gas industry to meet its Kyoto targets, it would simply have to shut down—no amount of tinkering could avoid it. The only way to avoid a total demolition of the industry would be to pay the ransom, as envisioned by Maurice Strong—a transfer of cash to the Third World, in exchange for their "rights" to emit carbon dioxide.

For the oil and gas industry to meet its Kyoto targets, it would simply have to shut down—no amount of tinkering could avoid it.

---

164 "A Discussion Paper on Canada's Contribution to Addressing Climate Change," Government of Canada, Ottawa, 2002, p. 15.

165 AMG, p. xv.

166 AMG, p. 9.

Strangely, one of the recommendations by AMG is that Canadians switch over their home furnaces, to burn more wood instead of coal or oil.[167] In fact, the government is counting on it—that switch will allegedly reduce 16 megatonnes of carbon dioxide a year. Trouble is, in order to cut down carbon dioxide, Canadians will have to cut down and burn a lot of trees, too—not exactly what most Greenpeace activists think of when they think of Kyoto. But Kyoto is not about trees, or rivers, or wildlife. It is about a fantastic battle against carbon dioxide, and if burning wood instead of natural gas achieves that goal, that's the plan. (Don't think your existing wood-burning fireplace is up to snuff, however; AMG specifically states that only "advanced combustion technology" furnaces that eliminate other emissions from wood burning will do.)

The depressing combination of all of this is the return of the 1970's phenomenon of stagflation—a decline in economic growth, coupled with rising prices. Incomes would fall; unemployment would climb. Normally when that happens the prices of goods fall, too. Not so under Kyoto: Inflation would be back with a vengeance—"two to three per cent higher"[168] than business as usual, the result of artificially high energy prices. Poorer Canadians would live in a more expensive economy.

AN ATTACK ON ENERGY

Canadian Manufacturers and Exporters, a leading industrial association, puts a local face on this national recession. They estimate that "more than 2,000 service sta-

---

[167] AMG, p. 45.

[168] AMG, p. 55.

tions across the country" would be closed—and the jobs that go with them would be lost. Of course, gas stations near the U.S. border—including every gas station in Toronto, Vancouver, Windsor and Montreal—would be especially hard hit. To fill up a 60-litre gas tank, who wouldn't drive an extra half hour across the U.S. border to save $30—and to fill up a few jerry cans along the way? And when 2,000 retail gas stations are shut down, that creates a domino effect back up the chain to marketers and refiners, too. The Canadian Manufacturers and Exporters estimates:

> a permanent loss of at least 12,000 jobs in Canada, a total that might be higher depending on the number of retail outlets shut down.[169]

Cross-border shopping—a phenomenon that faded as the Canadian dollar fell against the U.S. greenback—would be back with a vengeance. Canadian drivers would get their gasoline one way or another.

And that, on a family level, is exactly what will happen on a large industrial level, too. The U.S. will import oil, from one source or another.

On an industrial scale, U.S. energy consumers will do what penny-pinching Canadian car drivers will do—they will do their business in a non-Kyoto jurisdiction. The U.S. will simply import more oil from Venezuela and Mexico— or from a newly liberated Iraq. Auto production will be phased out of Canada, and into Michigan, or new auto-producing areas in the U.S. south. Canada's slavish adherence to the Kyoto treaty will cost Canadian families a lot, but it won't make the world any cleaner.

---

[169] Canadian Manufacturers and Exporters, *Pain Without Gain: Canada and the Kyoto Protocol*, p. 15.

This is the nasty surprise hidden in the Kyoto Trojan Horse. It is not just an attack on Alberta's oil patch, and the nascent oil rigs in Nova Scotia and Newfoundland. It is an attack on any Canadian who uses energy—or who builds things that use energy. "In order to achieve what the federal government is proposing," said Dr. Michael Walker of The Fraser Institute:

"We would have to have a reduction in energy intensity three times what we achieved as a result of the National Energy Program and the oil shocks following the Arab oil embargo."

> We would have to have a reduction in energy intensity three times what we achieved as a result of the National Energy Program and the oil shocks following the Arab oil embargo.[170]

But the oil shocks destroyed our standard of living, cost us money, and altered our lifestyle—why would we voluntarily sign up for such a program, especially when there is no environmental benefit to it at the end of the day?

---

[170] Michael Walker, *The National*, CBC, December 11, 1997.

CHAPTER TWELVE

Auto Manufacturing

The Canadian Manufacturers and Exporters association estimates that car production in Canada would decline by 8.2 per cent if Kyoto restrictions were in place. The government's AMG study is even more pessimistic: it predicts that the auto industry would fall by 13 per cent.[171]

Production of trucks would fall by 38.1 per cent compared to a Kyoto-free future. Approximately 4.8 per cent of auto workers would be laid off, as the industry would have $10-billion a year less to spend on wages and benefits.

This isn't a Western Canadian problem, like the old NEP was. It's a national problem—a new NEP that targets anything that needs fuel to stay warm or to move. As Gwyn Morgan, president of EnCana, Canada's largest industrial company, told the annual meeting of the Canadian Chamber of Commerce in London, Ontario:

> This is not an Ottawa versus Alberta, Saskatchewan and B.C. debate. It's Ottawa versus everywhere...
>
> It might seem like an Alberta issue, because we are in the hydrocarbon business and some of us have been vocal. But, Kyoto is as national an issue as they get. Sarnia is not

---

[171] AMG, p. 60.

in Alberta. Stelco is headquartered in Hamilton. GM in Oshawa. Ultramar is in Quebec. It goes on.[172]

Those thousands of lost auto jobs—the $80,000-a-year, bedrock-of-the-economy jobs? Eighty nine per cent of them are in Ontario. Another seven per cent are in Quebec. Kyoto's punishment of the auto industry is just as anti-Ontario as the NEP was anti-Alberta.

Janko Peric, the MP from Cambridge, is the chairman of the Liberal Auto Caucus, a group of MPs whose constituents rely on the auto sector for employment—in Peric's case, he has a Toyota plant in his riding. For many Auto Caucus MPs, it's personal—they rely on auto manufacturers for political contributions.

Kyoto's punishment of the auto industry is just as anti-Ontario as the NEP was anti-Alberta.

Peric says that all of the "Big Three" auto makers—General Motors, Ford and Chrysler—have expressed their concerns about Kyoto to him. "There have been some rumours that some of the plants may move down South,"[173] he admitted to *The Hill Times* newspaper, breaking the artificial silence of consensus that the Liberal caucus usually practices. Catching himself straying from the pro-Kyoto party line, Peric quickly labeled that industry threat "blackmail"—but the point was made. Auto plants have shut down before for smaller reasons than Kyoto.

---

172 Gwyn Morgan, "The Kyoto Accord or the Kyoto Discord?," address to Canadian Chamber of Commerce, September 24, 2002.

173 Mike Scandiffio, "Libs' Auto Caucus warn Prime Minister about ratifying Kyoto," *The Hill Times*, October 7, 2002.

Walt Lastewka, a Liberal MP from St. Catherines who used to work for GM, warns that any crash-course to reach Kyoto targets just doesn't fit with the auto industry's planning cycle necessary for redesigning cars, retooling factories and retraining workers. "What will the government do if the auto manufacturers don't meet the deadlines?" he asked *The Hill Times*. "Will there be penalties and if there are, then the cost of cars will go up and the consumer will have to pay." There is a tension in Lastewka's language; like his colleagues, Peric and Valeri, he wants to be a loyal Liberal, and be known as a supporter of "the environment"—for which Kyoto is illegitimately seen as the litmus test. But, like Peric and Valeri, he knows this deal makes no economic sense, and a lot of the people who support him will be hurt badly by it. His language isn't quite an attack on Kyoto; but it is an example of the cracks forming in the Liberal brick wall on the subject.

Ontario Liberal MP Roger Gallaway, whose Sarnia riding is home to an oil refinery, is the first to actually come out against Kyoto—at least until he sees the fine print. He said:

> I would vote against it because I do not know what the implications are. There's no committee hearings, there's no parliamentary scrutiny...
>
> You're being lulled into saying: 'I support Kyoto,' and then six months later, a budget bill comes that says we need $8 billion for Kyoto and you say: 'I don't want to support this.' It's deceptive.[174]

---

[174] Kate Jaimet, "Kyoto ratification slides in PM's favour," *Calgary Herald*, November 9, 2002, p. A6.

So far, though, none of Gallaway's colleagues have joined him in his Kyoto heresy—the closest would be Joe Comuzzi, the Liberal MP from Thunder Bay. He said:

> We can't do this thing without getting the provinces onside...We've got to listen to them. When we did the gun stuff, some of the provinces weren't onside, and we've had trouble ever since.[175]

Comuzzi isn't against Kyoto on any scientific or economic grounds—he just wants the provinces to sign off on it first. Gallaway and Comuzzi are heavily outnumbered, though. Just before Parliament reconvened in the fall of 2002, 119 Liberals—96 MPs and 23 Senators—signed a public letter to the Prime Minister urging him "to ratify the Kyoto Protocol in 2002."[176]

WHO DO THE UNIONS REALLY REPRESENT?

Canada's big unions are equally split on the subject. Ideologically, like the Liberal Party, they are naturally drawn to Kyoto, seeing in it the potential for massive government economic intervention in the economy—and with that, money for unionized workers. In July 2002, the Canadian Labour Congress formally endorsed Kyoto, saying that the deal actually isn't as strong as they'd like it to be—it "does less than is needed to address the issue of climate change." The CLC—Canada's umbrella organization for all labour unions—went on to demonize any opponents to Kyoto as "oil interests" who "will fight any limitation on their ability

---

[175] Kate Jaimet, "Kyoto ratification slides in PM's favour," *Calgary Herald*, November 9, 2002, p. A6.

[176] "119 Liberal caucus members support ratifying Kyoto in 2002," News release, Chicoutimi, August 22, 2002.

to continue to make super profits." The labour movement's official statement sounded like a class warfare call-to-arms from an earlier era. Endorsing Kyoto:

> seriously challenges the corporate agenda...and it strengthens the potential to build alliances with environmental movements based on a labour agenda.[177]

The CLC's rationale didn't sound like something that would be written by the typical union member in Canada in 2002—on average, a family man, working for an auto manufacturer in Ontario, earning $80,000-plus.

That knee-jerk endorsement of Kyoto based on socialist/environmentalist theory conflicts with the hard realities of Canada's auto sector. As the Canadian Auto Workers lobbyists complain:

> No one is building new auto plants here. Of 16 new assembly plants built or announced in North American since 1990, Canada has received only one.[178]

New plants aren't being built—and existing plants are being shut down. The CAW adds:

> We lost two plants during this same period (the Hyundai plant in Bromont, Quebec, and the GM van plant in Scarborough, Ontario), plus three more are facing closure.

These losses would happen just because of the general aspects of Kyoto—automobile factories would see their

---

[177] Canadian Auto Workers, "Health Safety and Environment Newsletter," Vol. 10, Number 4, July/August 2002.

[178] Canadian Auto Workers, "Left out in the cold: The Southward Migration of Auto Investment," Issues Sheet, 2002.

power bills skyrocket; car sales would slump as consumer demand would fall. But Ottawa is also mulling over a specific attack on sport utility vehicles—the most profitable pillar in the already shaky auto business.

In September 2002 a secretive committee of the federal cabinet met to look at the SUV tax, prompting concern from the Canadian Vehicle Manufacturers' Association. Mark Nantes, the president of the CVMA, told the *National Post* that such a tax—or any tax on new vehicles—actually hurts the environment, by discouraging consumers from upgrading to cleaner cars. Even trading in an old compact car for a new, full-sized SUV can result in less pollution—so any "sin tax" that hampers new car sales hurts the air as much as it hurts the economy. "Any time you increase the price of the vehicle, it ends up having a retarding effect," says Nantes. "It retards fleet turnover."[179]

Many pundits think that Kyoto will devastate Alberta—in fact, that is a reason why some of them like the treaty. But punishing the auto industry isn't an Alberta issue; it's as Ontario as they get.

And it's not just the auto workers. The Communications, Energy and Paperworkers Union has vigorously endorsed Kyoto—even though thousands of its members work in plants on Kyoto's hit list, from Hibernia's offshore oil rigs, to the Suncor oil sands plant in Alberta, to thousands of refinery workers in Ontario, Quebec and Alberta.[180] Like the CAW, the CEP complains that "between 1979 and 1998, 18 refineries were closed or downsized in Canada," but they still

---

179 Alan Toulin and Kate Jaimet, "Ottawa looks at 'sin tax' for SUVs," *National Post*, September 24, 2002, p. A4.

180 Communications, Energy and Paperworkers Union of Canada, "Energy Policy," 2002.

demand "mandatory targets" for reducing energy production in Canada. The CEP's policy paper—quite possibly the longest suicide letter ever written—admits that the last government adventure in energy, the National Energy Program, resulted in 27 plant closures, representing 12 per cent of the industry. Despite this, the CEP has no regrets, and blames free trade for the NEP's destruction. Do union members—whose dues pay for these anti-industry rants—know what their union bosses are saying on their behalf?

In September 2002 a secretive committee of the federal cabinet met to look at the SUV tax.

Union members have to decide what their union stands for. Is the purpose of the union to promote abstract 19th Century ideas of class warfare? Or is the purpose to look out for the workers' best financial interests—in this case, keeping factories and refineries in Canada, instead of losing them to Kyoto-exempt Mexico or the U.S.?

Unionized forestry workers might want to have a word with their union bosses, too. British Columbia—a province still struggling to get out of a politically-induced recession—has more to lose from Kyoto than most. Jock Finlayson,[181] executive director of the Business Council of British Columbia, asks:

> How do we know whether Ottawa will decide that B.C. forests have to be set aside from harvesting to absorb more carbon dioxide as part of Canada's greenhouse-gas commitment?

---

[181] Mike Byfield, "A question of sovereignty," *The Report*, October 21, 2002, p. 13.

Already B.C.'s once-vigorous lumber industry has been pygmified by U.S. tariffs, high taxes and the uncertainty of aboriginal land claims. Now the trees themselves might be held hostage, valued for their ability to consume carbon dioxide, a harmless gas. "We don't know. Kyoto is a black hole," he told *The Report* magazine in October 2002. Nearly five years after the Kyoto meeting—and despite a federal Environment Minister from B.C.—the province's forestry sector still has no clue about what Kyoto will mean for them.

Worried? Who wouldn't be?

CHAPTER THIRTEEN

Steel and Coal

The steel industry is another big loser under Kyoto. Like the auto industry, steel didn't taste the man-made recession of the NEP. But it will bear a heavy burden under Kyoto. Canadian steel manufacturers are already teetering on the edge of bankruptcy; foreign steel imports into Canada have doubled over the past decade—and all of that is without the added, artificial burdens of Kyoto.

Steel is an energy-thirsty industry, and so the absurd price-hikes that the government proposes for energy—remember, the "high price shocks" Canadians need to abstain from using energy—will hit steel towns such as Hamilton hard. Kyoto would tack on nine to 15 per cent to Canadian steel factories' costs—a final, and unexpected, stab in the back to an already battered industry. Thirty thousand job losses will hit Ontario alone, and another 5,000 will be gone in other provinces. The government's AMG study released in November 2000 predicted that Canada's iron and steel smelting industry would contract by 20 per cent, and non-ferrous smelting would decline by 12 per cent, too.[182]

---

[182] AMG, p. 59.

Tony Valeri, the Liberal MP from Stoney Creek, Ontario, chairs the multi-party Steel Caucus[183]—a group of 25 pro-industry MPs, similar to the Auto Caucus. Like Peric, Valeri has violated the Liberal party's cone of silence about Kyoto's effect on industry, too. "Additional costs [cannot be] passed on to the customer, not to the U.S." he says—U.S. customers will simply buy from other suppliers who do not have extra Kyoto costs, such as higher energy bills, or Kyoto regulations, such as emissions reductions or mandatory operating "credits" to be purchased from Third World countries.

No doubt the mayor of Pittsburgh will declare "Kyoto Day" to be a civic holiday, the day that Canada's government did more for U.S. steelmakers than any Pennsylvania Senator ever could.

Needless to say, steel companies in the U.S. will be more than willing to pick up the slack. No doubt the mayor of Pittsburgh will declare "Kyoto Day" to be a civic holiday—the day that Canada's government did more for U.S. steelmakers than any Pennsylvania Senator ever could. John Godfrey, a blindly pro-Kyoto Liberal MP, doesn't care. "The United States is not monolithic, there is enough business in the progressive states,"[184] he argued—"progressive," it seems, being Godfrey's definition of U.S. businesses that would willingly pay more than the going rate for steel.

Of course, if steel mills are shut down, iron ore mining will fall, too—by a full 30 per cent, according to AMG.

---

[183] Mike Scandiffio, "Libs' Auto Caucus warn Prime Minister about ratifying Kyoto," *The Hill Times*, October 7, 2002.

[184] Scandiffio, 2002.

Rubber and plastic products manufacturing will tumble 15 per cent. And even electronic products—not usually thought of as vulnerable to the energy-oriented Kyoto Protocol—will fall back 17 per cent.

After rattling off these Depression-era figures, the AMG government report writes "The coal industry is the one industry that will face significant deterioration...from 40 to 50 per cent." This is a staggering fact—half of all people in the Canadian coal industry will be out of work. But just as staggering is the blasé attitude of the government economists. "Forty to 50 per cent" is "significant," they write; apparently the 20 per cent-range layoffs throughout the rest of Canada's industrial heartland don't warrant the phrase "significant." For a little splash of reality, recall that the technical definition of a recession is just six months in a row where the economy shrinks; in 1931, in the middle of the Great Depression, Canada's economy shrank by 11 per cent.[185] Kyoto would throw Canadian industry into a Great Depression—but unlike the Dirty Thirties, the United States would not suffer along with us.

Energy, automobiles, steel—all of these are heavy industries, but for the most part rely on physical plants that can be relocated to the U.S. However, some industries targeted by Kyoto simply can't be moved. They'll be trapped, trying to survive under a confusing patchwork of taxes, regulations and government programs.

---

[185] Centre for the Study of Living Standards, *Personal Income Trends in the 1990s*, September 25, 1997.

CHAPTER FOURTEEN

Transportation

Unlike tiny Monaco, which has also signed Kyoto, travelling from one end of Canada to the other uses energy. And if you want to move people or products around Canada, you have to do it in Canada—you can't move that business to the U.S. So what can Canadian truckers and other transporters do about Kyoto?

According to Statistics Canada, one of the strongest areas of jobs growth has been in the truck and transportation industry[186]—a glimmer in an otherwise glum economy. But trucking and transportation are energy-intensive industries, producing more greenhouse gas emissions than any other sector, including electrical plants or even oil and gas fossil fuel production. In other words, the most hopeful source of new employment in Canada right now is the one that will be hit the hardest by Kyoto.

David Collenette, the federal Transport Minister, does not seem to be shy about sacrificing the industry he is supposed to protect. After the Liberal Throne Speech, Collenette gave a private interview to *The Toronto Star* in which he outlined the Liberal plan to force businesses to

---

[186] Statistics Canada, Labour Force Survey, September 2002.

ship goods on trains and boats, instead of on trucks. "Kyoto plan to take trucks off the 401" screamed the *Star's* banner headline—a message met with joy, no doubt, by many motorists happy to have anyone else taken off the road.[187] Less jubilant would be the truckers and others in Toronto's massive distribution and transportation system. How do you ship VCRs from Markham to Etobicoke by boat?

Like most of the details about Kyoto's implementation, confusion reigns. According to the *Star's* report on Collenette's private briefing:

> The federal plan would shift more truck traffic to rail and water...freeing up the overtaxed Highway 401 for carpooling.

If Collenette gets his way, it will be illegal to go for a drive on the 401 without taking along a neighbour, too.

Perhaps the motorists who cheered the headline's news of truckers being banned should have read that small print: If Collenette gets his way, it will be illegal to go for a drive on the 401 without taking along a neighbour, too.

For some reason, Collenette didn't choose to share with Star readers his other plan for the 401: toll booths. According to a Kyoto discussion paper published by the government in 2002, "road pricing" would be necessary to make people drive less. "Road-tolls on major inter-city and urban highways" would be used to decrease car travel enough to reduce carbon dioxide emissions by 2.7 megatonnes. To price many poorer drivers off the road, Ottawa

---

187 Tim Harper and Less Whittington, "Kyoto plan to take trucks off the 401," *The Toronto Star*, October 1, 2002, p. A1.

estimates that this would require "a 10 per cent cost increase for inter-city travel and up to 100 per cent for urban travel."[188] It turns out that for-profit truckers might be the only people able to afford to go for a drive in the future.

Collenette will take tens of thousands of trucks off the road—and hundreds of thousands of single-passenger cars, too. How that part of the plan will happen is not too hard to imagine: No doubt, hundreds of RCMP officers will be taken off less-important beats and put on Traffic Patrol—ticketing single-passenger cars, and pulling over anything larger than a mini-van. Remember, Ottawa always said that Kyoto would pay. Less easy to imagine, however, would be how Ontario's industry could substitute "rail and water" transport for trucks.

Just to take one small example, how would farmers replace refrigerator trucks, which right now take food from their farms to grocery warehouses? How would trains or boats work from land-locked farmers fields, miles from any railway spur? And what—if not refrigerated trucks—would then ship produce from the warehouse to a hundred Toronto grocery stores?

The impracticality of eliminating trucks in this one niche—refrigerated food—can be multiplied a hundredfold, for every good that needs to be moved from factory to retailer. Even goods that are already transported by train and ship need to be eventually off-loaded onto trucks to go to their final destination.

Don't bother Minister Collenette with these trivial objections, though. "We have to do this," he says. "It's

---

188 "A Discussion Paper on Canada's Contribution to Addressing Climate Change," Government of Canada, Ottawa, 2002, p. 51.

being done in Europe and more and more, it is being done in the U.S."

Actually, no it's not. The Kyoto Protocol doesn't require Europe to reduce its emissions much, if at all—because countries that might have to reduce their emissions on their own, like Belgium, can balance off against other European countries with room to spare under Kyoto. And, even if it did, would it make sense to model Canada's transportation system—designed to traverse the second-largest country in the world—after postage-stamp-size statelets such as Luxembourg and Lichtenstein?

Would it make sense to model Canada's transportation system—designed to traverse the second-largest country in the world—after postage-stamp-size statelets such as Luxembourg and Lichtenstein?

Contrary to Collenette's assertion, the U.S. is building more highways and trucks as fast as it can. Only Canada has cooked up the no-trucks plan. "Plan," however, is too strong a word. As the *Star* noted, Collenette "did not place a price tag on the program."

The trucking industry won't just be gutted because it burns fuel, like cars do. It will be hit hard because many of the industries that require trucking will be decimated as well. Take Ward Chemical Inc., a mid-sized business that maintains gravel roads for the oil patch, and provides salty brine that is used to stop oil wells from turning into "gushers."

Ward itself is not likely to come under inspection by Kyotocrats—its main product is naturally occurring salt water, not carbon dioxide. To be sure, Ward's own costs will rise, at it bears the burden of extra taxes on the energy it uses for processing its brine, and for fuelling its trucks. But by far the bigger impact is the loss of Ward's main customers: the oil and gas industry.

According to Al Korchinski, Ward's president, the company's workforce balloons by up to 100 extra contractors during the busy season—mainly jobs driving trucks of his product around the province. If the oil business takes a hit, so will dozens of Korchinski's truckers. "We are tied to the success of these prime industries. If they become inactive, so do we,"[189] he says.

Most drivers, of course, are not truckers, but ordinary families with cars—and those family cars are responsible for more greenhouse gases than all heavy-duty trucks and buses, railways and ships combined.[190] Of course, it is easier to sell Kyoto as an attack on truckers than on the family car—but as Collenette warned the *Star*, once the truck-banning starts, forced car-pooling won't be far behind.

---

[189] Al Korchinski, personal interview, October 29, 2002.

[190] Canadian Manufacturers and Exporters, *Pain Without Gain: Canada and the Kyoto Protocol*, p. 5.

CHAPTER FIFTEEN

Agriculture

"Agriculture contributes 10 to 13 per cent of Canada's greenhouse gas emissions,"[191] according to the federal government. It's a large percentage of Canada's total emissions, a fact that likely comes as a surprise to many who think Kyoto is a problem only for the energy sector, or big Ontario factories.

By coincidence, one of the Canadian MPs who has led the charge for agriculture against Kyoto is David L. Anderson, from Cypress Hills—Grasslands, Saskatchewan, not to be confused with David Anderson, the Environment Minister from Victoria, and Canada's chief Kyoto booster. In the battle of the David Andersons, the Saskatchewanian has compiled a long list of key questions for his nemesis— questions that no environment minister has answered in the five years since Kyoto was signed.

Will Kyoto result in higher consumer food prices? How much will Canadian agricultural exports decline as a result? How many farmers will we lose as a result of Kyoto? And—the most obvious question—how will the

---

191 R.L. Desjardins and R. Riznek, "Agricultural Greenhouse Gas Budget, *Environmental Sustainability of Canadian Agriculture*, Agriculture and Agri-Food Canada, Ottawa, 2000, p. 134.

government manage the resulting increase in demand for public assistance for farmers?[192]

Reducing Kyoto emissions in agriculture would have a devastating effect on an industry that is already being battered by foreign subsidies and trade barriers. If Canadian farmers had to reduce greenhouse gases, but U.S. farmers didn't, "the hog industry in Canada could reduce exports by 23 to 47 per cent."[193] This is not because the hog industry or any other agricultural endeavour emits massive amounts of carbon dioxide—in fact, agriculture accounts for only about four per cent of all Canadian carbon dioxide emissions.[194] Instead, it is because agriculture does account for a disproportionate amount of some of Canada's other greenhouse gases, such as methane and nitrous oxide—41 per cent and 66 per cent respectively. Those gases' chemical properties give them, pound for pound, much more concentrated impact than carbon dioxide.

Reducing Kyoto emissions in agriculture would have a devastating effect on an industry that is already being battered by foreign subsidies and trade barriers.

For Canadian hog farmers—a growing industry—there is just no way to turn the emissions clock back to 1990 levels, less six per cent as the Kyoto Protocol demands. The only other

---

192 David L. Anderson, *Kyoto and Canadian Agriculture*, October 28, 2002, p. 9.

193 Richard Gray, Debora Harper and Tim Highmoore, *Greenhouse Gas Policies and the International Competitiveness of the Hog Industry*, as presented to the International Agricultural Trade Research Consortium, Auckland, New Zealand, January 2001, p. 16.

194 Gray, Harper and Highmoore, p. 4.

practical option is for farmers to buy "emissions credits" from Third World countries, to allow their hogs to continue to "emit" their methane. It is that artificial cost that will roll back Canadian pork exports by nearly half—and possibly make Canadian pork uneconomical even for Canadian consumers.

BELCHING AND FLATULENCE

Possibly the least popular assignment in Canada's Agriculture Department these days is euphemistically called the "belching and flatulence" directorate. That's where civil servants spend countless hours—and tax dollars—capturing and analyzing animal burps and farts. To cut down on the giggling, departmental staff, including the Minister, refer to these as "livestock emissions," but there's no getting around it: Our government believes that in order to meet our Kyoto obligations, we have to make cattle and sheep toot less. It's no small thing—according to the government, emissions from animals and their manure make up 20 megatonnes of greenhouse gases each year[195]—fully one twelfth the amount Canada must cut back to meet Kyoto's targets.

To aid in this utopian quest, Ottawa has sponsored many creative initiatives. ManureNet, for example, is an official government website tackling this sensitive subject in both official languages.[196] No word yet as to how many cows have made the site their Internet home page.

---

[195] R.L. Desjardins and R. Riznek, "Agricultural Greenhouse Gas Budget," *Environmental Sustainability of Canadian Agriculture*, Agriculture and Agri-Food Canada, Ottawa, 2000, p. 133.

[196] On-line posting. ManureNet.
<http://res2.agr.ca/initiatives/manurenet/>

One desperate study, done in Manitoba and posted on ManureNet, suggests that cattle should take drugs to stop farting.[197] According to this study, dairy cows that had an additive called monensin mixed into their diets farted up to 28 per cent less, according to scientists, who claim to have actually measured. Trouble is, "the impact has not been [as] long lasting," as scientists had hoped. Other ideas suggested by scientists include pumping cattle full of anti-farting hormones, such as Bovine somatotropin,[198] which cut down on methane emissions by nine per cent. But even the most ardent anti-farting scientists on the Kyoto payroll are skeptical about jacking up cattle on hormones, just to make them more polite.

Ottawa's high-stakes race to solve the problem of musical cattle—reminiscent of the grandeur of John Kennedy's Apollo project, or the search for the polio vaccine—has electrified the country. It has also polarized the electorate, with both pro- and anti-farting factions making themselves heard.

On the anti-farting side proudly stands Environmental Defence Canada, an eco-activist group dedicated to fart-free

---

[197] R.G. Kinsman et al., "Methane and carbon dioxide emissions in lactating Holsteins," *Dairy Research Report*, Centre for Food and Animal Research, Agriculture and Agri-Food Canada, 1997 as cited by Karin Wittenberg and Dinah Boadi, "Reducing Greenhouse Gas Emissions From Livestock Agriculture in Manitoba," presentation to Manitoba Climate Change Taskforce, Public Consultation Sessions, May 11, 2001.

[198] Karin Wittenberg and Dinah Boadi, "Reducing Greenhouse Gas Emissions From Livestock Agriculture in Manitoba," presentation to Manitoba Climate Change Taskforce, Public Consultation Sessions, May 11, 2001.

living. In October 2002, they released a scathing 37-page report called *It's Hitting the Fan*—pointing out that cattle and pigs nearly outnumber people in Canada, and all of those animals are farting—creating "foul odours," "toxic vapours" and even cause "headaches."[199] Who could argue with that?

Bob Friesen would, that's who. He's the president of the Canadian Federation of Agriculture, and his group fired back with their own press release,[200] entitled *Environment Group Spreads Manure*.

It was the flatulence debate's equivalent of Muhammed Ali versus Joe Frazier.

Maybe environmentalists should look after their own farts before pointing fingers at pigs and cattle.

"When it comes to harmful bacteria," argued Friesen, "a farm of 10,000 hogs produces as much fecal coliform bacteria as a population of 2,300 people." The subtext of Friesen's riposte was clear: Maybe environmentalists should look after their own farts before pointing fingers at pigs and cattle.

Friesen then pressed his advantage. He said:

> Animals produce manure, manure is spread on the land to grow crops, and animals eat the crops. It's a perfectly natural and beneficial cycle.

---

[199] Amie Fulton, Burkhard Mausberg and Michelle Campbell, "It's Hitting the Fan," Environmental Defence Canada, Toronto, October 2002.

[200] Canadian Federation of Agriculture, "Environment Group Spreads Manure," Ottawa, October 4, 2002.

After all, without natural manure, farmers would need artificial chemicals.

What Friesen didn't mention was that 150 years ago, while there were fewer cattle and pigs in Canada, 60 million farting, burping buffalo roamed the prairies.[201]

At first, it's hard to understand how a few million cattle can emit as much greenhouse gas as a few million cars. The answer lies in science: The main Kyoto gas emitted by cars is carbon dioxide, but the main Kyoto gas emitted by cattle is methane. Over a twenty-year period, each molecule of methane contributes 56 times as much warmth as a carbon dioxide molecule does.[202] The scientific term for this is "global warming potential." So, over twenty years, one pound of cow farts causes as much warming as 56 pounds of carbon dioxide from automobile emissions. Kyoto counts methane at equivalent to 21 times carbon dioxide. But even that flatulence discount means that the rude emissions of cows, pigs and other livestock emit more Kyoto gases (27.4 megatonnes) than all Canadian steel mills (8.5 megatonnes), more than all waste incinerators in the country (a paltry 0.35 megatonnes), and more than all airplanes (13.6 megatonnes)—more than all of these combined. Livestock, in fact, emits more than half as much Kyoto gas as all the cars in Canada do.[203]

---

201 Will Verboven, "Science of Kyoto bends both ways," *Calgary Herald*, November 3, 2002, p. A13.

202 U.S. Environmental Protection Agency, "Greenhouse Gases and Global Warming Potential Values," excerpt from the *Inventory of U.S. Greenhouse Emissions and Sinks*: 1990-2000, April, 2002.

203 "Canada's 1999 Greenhouse Gas Emission Summary," Environment Canada, Ottawa, 2001.

FERTILIZERS

Another related agricultural industry is that of fertilizers—not something that most politicians on Parliament Hill probably think about, but a massive Canadian industry nonetheless. Twelve thousand Canadians work directly in the fertilizer business, accounting for $2.5-billion in domestic sales and $3.2-billion in exports—meeting 12 per cent of the world's supply.[204]

Since 1990—the year of record for Kyoto—Canada's production of fertilizers have increased dramatically, by more than 38 per cent in the case of nitrogen-based fertilizers. The growth in greenhouse gas emissions, however, has only been around 33 per cent. As the Canadian industry has grown, it has become more efficient.[205]

Like Canada's efficient oil and gas sector, if Canadian fertilizers are suddenly tagged with additional costs—either through Kyoto taxes, higher input costs or having to buy imaginary "emissions credits" from the Third World—then Canada's foreign buyers will simply purchase their fertilizers from the United States, or the Middle East, neither of which will be bound by Kyoto. The end result will actually be more pollution, not less—but Canadian jobs will be lost in the process. Foreign countries who still bought more expensive fertilizer from Canada would be paying more money to grow food—not exactly a socially responsible strategy.

Of course, the cost of fertilizer is one of the costs that go into a farmer's budget; higher fertilizer costs add yet another trouble to Canadian farmers—in addition to

---

[204] Canadian Fertilizer Institute, *Science-Based Decisions*, Ottawa, March 2000, p. 18.

[205] Canadian Fertilizer Institute, p. 4.

European and American subsidies, and the cost of Kyoto fuel taxes, too. A U.S. study written by several scientists, including Terry Francl, the senior economist and commodity specialist at the American Farm Bureau Federation, estimated that a 50-cent-per-gallon tax hike—slightly more than 10 cents per litre—would gut farmers' profits across the board. U.S. wheat farmers would have their profits plunge by more than 57 per cent based on a 10-cent-per-litre fuel tax hike alone. Dairy farmers would lose more than 53 per cent of their profits, too. Corn farmers would see their profits fall by 47 per cent. And hog farmers—not a robust industry to begin with—would see profits fall by 84 per cent.[206]

Those are American studies; Canadian farmers already trudge along with higher tax burdens than their American cousins. But even if the impact on Canadian farmers was only half as severe, thousands of farmers who are already on the edge of bankruptcy would be tipped over, thanks to Kyoto.

---

[206] Terry Francl, Richard Nadler and Joseph Bast, "Impact of the Kyoto Protocol on Agriculture," American Council for Capital Formation Center for Policy Research, October, 1998.

◇ **CHAPTER SIXTEEN**

Concealing the True Costs of Kyoto

The federal government knows that Kyoto will cost a lot; it has commissioned countless studies, including the one admitting that Kyoto will cause a made-in-Ottawa recession. But rather than putting these cost estimates before the public for a hearty debate, the Environment Minister has engaged in a cover-up that would make Richard Nixon blush.

Take the federal government's Kyoto cabinet meetings in September 2002. Two different high-powered committees of ministers were meeting to make decisions about Kyoto—the economic development committee, and the social union committee. But, before the ministers were able to read their briefing notes, embarrassing government estimates as to the costs were expunged from the record. Government bureaucrats had moved from hiding the truth about Kyoto from the Canadian public, to hiding it from even the most senior politicians in the country.

Those blacked-out passages were obtained by the *National Post*, which ran them as an exclusive on their front page.[207] According to the leaked information that the

---

[207] Alan Toulin, "Kyoto cost hidden from Cabinet," *National Post*, September 25, 2002, p. A1.

Post received, "the largest economic impacts will be felt in Alberta and Ontario"—putting a lie to Ottawa's pledge that Kyoto would not discriminate against any particular region. Alberta is used to this sort of economic bullying. But to Ontario—a province that has dutifully sent a hundred Liberal MPs to Ottawa in each of the last three elections—being singled out for economic punishment must come as a shocking surprise, and a betrayal of a political compact. According to the government's AMG study, "Ontario accounts for more than one-half of all lasting negative effects on the Canadian economy."[208] At least Ottawa could argue that Alberta had it coming—for the last three elections, that province has voted overwhelmingly against Jean Chrétien and the Liberals. But what did the auto industry and the steel industry ever do to deserve this?

The blacked-out cabinet documents conceded that the economy would lose 200,000 jobs and shave 1.5 per cent off GDP growth. Cabinet ministers were deliberately kept in the dark about the Kyoto recession.

Like it was to the voters of Ontario, this sort of skullduggery must have been an unpleasant surprise to Liberal cabinet ministers who only learned about the wool being pulled over their eyes in the next morning's paper. After all, keeping the opposition parties in the dark is expected—perhaps even normal, for a government. But to deliberately hide the dangers of Kyoto *from Liberal cabinet ministers themselves* is a level of trickery rarely seen in Canada.

Occasionally, however, the truth does get out—despite Ottawa's official policy of Kyoto secrecy. Sometimes the truth gets out in the form of an anonymous manila envelope,

---

[208] AMG, p. 62.

sent to a reporter by a concerned civil servant. And, once in a while, political researchers in an opposition party get their hands on secret government information, too.

It is a sad statement about the practices of the Liberal government that merely revealing an apolitical economic study can cause a scandal—in more accountable democracies, government economic studies are not considered to be private political dynamite, to be hoarded and kept secret from one's rivals. Rather, as in the United States and Australia, this sort of public information is shared without regard for petty partisan interests.

In more accountable democracies, government economic studies are not considered to be private political dynamite, to be hoarded and kept secret from one's rivals.

On February 28, 2002, John Reynolds, then the leader of the Canadian Alliance, exposed to the House of Commons one of the secret economic impact studies that the Environment Minister had kept under wraps. That report stated: "Kyoto will cost Canadians up to $75-billion in lost revenue" thundered Reynolds. "Will the Environment Minister still insist on ratifying the Kyoto treaty?" he asked.

David Anderson, the Environment Minister, knew about the study as well—he had been briefed about it before Question Period, as all ministers are on the hot topics of the day. Every Minister has a daily briefing book prepared by their department's spin doctors and their personal staff. Those briefing books contain relevant stories from the morning papers, and a report as to the latest "buzz" in the parliamentary press gallery. But the briefing books also contain warnings for the minister about potentially embarrassing facts that could be sprung on them at any time—and the suggested reply for the minister.

These briefing books are read over and over by ministers, and ministers often go through practice "dress rehearsals" of Question Period, especially when they are under daily attack. So when Reynolds blasted Anderson with the $75-billion figure, Anderson had a ready reply.

"Mr. Speaker," said the minister rather sheepishly, "the honourable Leader of the Opposition has once again misrepresented a study done for the Industry Department."

"It is a working paper," Anderson explained. "It is working paper number 34. There are 33 others before it."

Anderson gave his response with his trademark hauteur, and his fellow government MPs applauded on cue, the hallmark of well-trained back-benchers. But had they actually considered the importance of his statement—especially the two-thirds of Anderson's caucus colleagues who hail from Ontario—they probably would have clapped with as little enthusiasm as the party whip would allow.

Anderson's reply conceded Reynolds' point. The minister admitted that, indeed, government economists had estimated Kyoto's cost at a whopping $75-billion—nearly twice the dollar amount of even the most pessimistic studies. For comparison, $75-billion is more than Ottawa rakes in each year from the GST; it's larger than the entire economies of Uganda and Yemen—combined.[209]

It's $10,000 for every Canadian family of four.

---

[209] *The World Factbook* 2002. On-line posting. Central Intelligence Agency. <http://www.cia.gov>

But not to worry, Anderson says. It is a working paper—precisely the kind of working paper that Anderson's bureaucrats censored from his presentation to cabinet.

Kyoto costs more than even its most pessimistic opponents can imagine. The government knows it. And the government doesn't care. It cares more about covering up the costs, than actually dealing with them. Spin is more important than substance. And the hundred Liberal backbenchers from Ontario pound their desks on demand, and get ready to sign an agreement that will throw untold thousands of their own constituents out of work. Bravo.

Kyoto costs more than even its most pessimistic opponents can imagine. The government knows it.

Anderson was only following in Parliament's abysmal tradition of meaningless discussions of the facts of global warming—going back to the long-since-fired Christine Stewart, the minister who boastfully boarded that fateful flight to Kyoto, Japan in 1997, bragging that she would sign any deal that was cooked up, no matter the cost—as long as Canada bested the U.S. in terms of carbon emission reductions. Well, Stewart achieved her dubious goal, the U.S. Senate has unanimously refused to ratify the treaty, and her hapless successor is left scrambling to explain why $75-billion has to be diverted away from education, health care and the Canadian armed forces.

CHAPTER SEVENTEEN

Kyoto and Kyoto Lite

Fighting Kyoto requires a fighting spirit—but, with the exception of a few gallant pockets of resistance, Canadians are either unaware of Kyoto's dangers, unsure of how to fight back, or unconvinced that they can win.

Unfortunately, that is the stereotypical Canadian way—moderation and caution in all things. The trouble is Kyoto's proponents are playing by a different set of rules. They have been implementing their own political battle plan for five years, and have inexorably moved the Kyoto Protocol from a diplomat's fantasy to a practical reality.

With Madison Avenue-calibre marketing and Maoist determination, they have won every battle they have fought, from putting Canada's signature on the deal in 1997 without telling Parliament what it would cost, to putting forward a motion to ratify without provincial consultation. And now all of a sudden it is being implemented—all of a sudden having taken five years.

For five years, skeptics and opponents of Kyoto have played by the Marquis of Queensbury rules. Even Alberta—a province used to bucking Ottawa's edicts—has been cautious in its opposition.

Part of that caution is because of the natural risk-aversion of politicians and businessmen alike. In the years when Kyoto was just an environmental slogan, it was superbly popular with the electorate. What politician would speak against clean air and water—the masterful propaganda of activists who successfully managed to keep questions like "how much will it cost?" and "will it really help the environment?" out of the discussion. For five years, anti-Kyoto politicians were cautious because it did not make sense to take political flak for sounding anti-environmentalist by fighting against a foreign treaty that might never be implemented.

As Guy Giorno, the former chief of staff to Ontario Premier Mike Harris notes, Canadian public opinion is blissfully ignorant about the potential economic impacts of signing the treaty. Giorno points to a major opinion poll conducted for the Quebec Chamber of Commerce in September 2002 which showed that 81 per cent of Canadians support Kyoto—but 51 per cent of Canadians had not even heard of Kyoto before. "We have no idea what it is, but we love it anyway," Giorno wrote, in a rare anti-Kyoto column in *The Toronto Star.*

> The most significant economic policy since free trade apparently depends on the support of people who think the Kyoto Protocol is a sushi bar.[210]

In Alberta, a poll by Environics West shows that fully 91 per cent of the public had heard of Kyoto, but fully 45 per cent were unfamiliar with it[211]—this, in the home of the most anti-Kyoto provincial government in the country.

---

[210] Guy Giorno, "Quick fixes don't work," *The Toronto Star,* September 8, 2002, p. A13.

[211] "Polling shows most Albertans support a made-in-Canada alternative to Kyoto," News release, Government of Alberta, October 4, 2002.

Canadian businesses have reason to be cautious in their opprobrium, too: any company that is regulated by the federal government can only go so far in criticizing that government before it is punished. Airlines, auto manufacturers, oil and gas companies, exporters—even banks and brokerage houses—live and die at the whim of the federal government. An oil and gas company that needs to keep in the good books of the National Energy Board would be wise not to offend the Minister of Energy who appoints the officers to that board.

Risk aversion is not the only problem in the current fight-back strategy. Canadians have adopted an attitude of constitutional inferiority when it comes to government fiats.

Risk aversion is not the only problem in the current fight-back strategy. Canadians have adopted an attitude of constitutional inferiority and fatalism when it comes to government fiats, especially those from Ottawa. After all, the federal government did not consult Canadians before it signed or moved to ratify Kyoto as it promised it would—why would it restrain itself now?

In the summer of 2002, the federal Environment Department did indeed hold public hearings about whether or not Canada should ratify Kyoto. "Public hearings" might be a bit of a stretch, actually. Ottawa consulted only with Canadians who met Ottawa's official criterion of being part of "interested and well-informed stakeholder groups that have specific interest in and expertise on climate change." Kyoto skeptics—including nationally-respected scientists and economists—were excluded. Lobbyists from the Sierra Club, however, were invited to make presentations in five different cities.[212] Like Parliament itself, where backbench MPs merely follow the Prime Minister's scripts, these "consultations" were merely for show. What company—or provincial government— would want to get in the way of such a juggernaut, lumbering towards a foregone conclusion?

ALBERTA'S KYOTO LITE

Shut out of true consultations, targeted with personal insults and facing a federal government clearly on the Kyoto warpath, Alberta decided to switch gears. On October 17, 2002, the Government of Alberta announced its own greenhouse emissions reduction plan.[213]

It was a tactical move that made some political sense— polling, including the province's own internal polls, showed that while Canadians were skeptical of a made-in-Japan treaty, they did want their governments to take some steps at reducing greenhouse gas emissions. By proposing an Alberta plan—even before the federal government proposed its own—the province could take the initiative, and mitigate the public impression that Alberta was completely uninterested in the environment, and completely focused on producing as much fossil fuel as possible.

The gambit worked, at least in some respects. It caught the federal government off guard; it put the Kyoto lobbyists on the defensive, who probably wound up coming across to many Canadians as excessively purist for rejecting the Alberta proposal out of hand. It also added a new spin to

---

212 Lorne Gunter, "No room for the public in Liberals' royal court," *Edmonton Journal*, July 21, 2002, p. A10.

213 *Taking Action*, Government of Alberta, October, 2002.

the media discussion: a "made in Canada plan," something that naturally sounded appealing. And it gave other provinces something constructive and positive to attach themselves to, rather than merely opposing Ottawa's ideas.

From an economic point of view, the Alberta plan has its advantages. The emissions reductions contemplated within it are not on the crash-course schedule of Kyoto. Whereas Kyoto demands gas reductions be achieved by 2012 at the latest, the Alberta plan is scheduled to hit its stride in the year 2020 and beyond.

The Alberta model completely abandons the Kyoto idea of fixed quota emissions, within which any jurisdiction must remain, no matter how its population or economy grows.

Another important difference is that the Alberta model completely abandons the Kyoto idea of a fixed quota of emissions, within which any jurisdiction must remain, no matter how its population or economy grows. Instead, Alberta's plan aims to reduce the "intensity" of greenhouse emissions. For every dollar worth of energy produced, for example, Alberta plans to emit fewer gases. If Alberta's production of oil and gas doubles over the next decade, for example, the Alberta plan would seek to have the emissions grow by less than double. Kyoto, on the other hand, makes no provision for an expanding economy; quotas are fixed.

In other ways, however, the Alberta plan concedes certain arguments. It does not dispute the scientific theory that the Earth is warming, nor the theory that man-made emissions are causing that warming. It does not address the fact that carbon dioxide and methane emissions are not pollution by the normal definition of that word. And, although the Alberta plan is less restrictive, it carries with it "financial consequences"[214] for companies that fail to meet its targets—something that the federal version has yet to spell out, though it likely will.

While the federal government was quick to attack the Alberta plan as too watered down—Kyoto Lite—some of the most ardent Kyoto critics condemned the Alberta plan as conceding every argument against implementing Kyoto—and haggling only over the degree of implementation. The Alberta Alliance, a nascent provincial political party to the right of Ralph Klein's Tories, seized upon the Alberta plan, calling it a "made-in-Alberta National Energy Program" and that the Premier had "surrendered to Ottawa without a fight."[215]

Not all Kyoto critics agree with that analysis. "In political terms, Alberta's Kyoto Lite, coupled with its P.R. campaign, has been brilliant,"[216] says columnist Lorne Gunter, one of Canada's leading Kyoto skeptics.

> It has transformed public opinion in Alberta by 45 points in three months—or at least contributed to that enormous shift. And I even think it contributed to the shift nationally, to the point now where public opinion on Kyoto is evenly divided.

But even though Gunter points out the short-term political benefits of the Alberta plan, he worries that by

---

[214] *Taking Action*, Government of Alberta, October, 2002, p. 2.

[215] Randy Thorsteinson, "Klein's plan belligerent towards oil-patch," *Edmonton Journal*, October 21, 2002, p. A15.

[216] Lorne Gunter, personal interview, November 12, 2002.

coming up with a plan at all, for a problem that may not even exist in science, could do long-term harm to Alberta's cause. "Alberta should never have conceded the science behind global warming theory," he says. "It will someday regret having done so. But its campaign dealt the politics of Kyoto a major body blow."

Lee Morrison, the former MP who vociferously opposed Kyoto in the House of Commons, was equally upset. "The government of Alberta has endorsed the theology of human-induced global warming,"[217] he wrote. By admitting that emissions do harm the planet, warned Morrison, the argument that "remedial action must be delayed for economic reasons" is rendered "untenable."

> **"Alberta should never have conceded the science," says Lorne Gunter. "It will someday regret having done so."**

Be that as it may, the release of the Alberta plan lit a fire under the feds—and another angry outburst from David Anderson showed he wasn't happy with it. He sneered:

> We've always said we suspected there was a strong Houston oil interest, read: Exxon, involvement in the Alberta plan.

When Premier Klein announced that he was traveling to the U.S. to sell his made-in-Alberta plan, Anderson was left scrambling. He said:[218]

---

217 Lee Morrison, "Has Alberta fallen victim to Kyoto fever?," *Calgary Herald*, November 9, 2002, p. OS7.

218 Tom Olsen and Rick Mofina, "Grits condemn Klein mission," *Calgary Herald*, November 9, 2002, p. A1.

Alberta's a great place for Americans to invest in now, and it'll be a great place to invest in the oil and gas industry, even after ratification of Kyoto.

DAVID ANDERSON'S PLAN

Exactly a week after Alberta released its plan, Anderson released his "draft plan"[219]—essentially a few dozen PowerPoint slides, rehashing the same ideas that had been bandied about by Kyotocrats for five years. Much of the "draft plan" was a dumbed-down recap of the scientific theories behind Kyoto—not the definition of a plan, but necessary to fill up some space in a paltry document.

It is the kind of "draft plan" that is a bureaucrat's delight, but would cause any business person trying to make a decision pull out his hair. Chock full of buzzwords and New Age bureaucratese, it is nothing less than a 48-page admission that the Department of Environment—with 4,000 bureaucrats and a half-billion dollar budget—has not done a thing over the past five years since Kyoto to prepare for implementing the treaty. It isn't even written out in full sentences. It's a collection of phrases, in point form, on a series of slides. What self-respecting cabinet minister would release a "draft plan" like that?

What does this mean: "Create international credits with good rates of return"?[220] Does that constitute a plan?

Or this: "Clarify architecture as soon as possible"?[221] Or this:

---

[219] *Climate Change Draft Plan*, Government of Canada, 2002.

[220] Government of Canada, p. 16.

[221] Government of Canada, p. 20.

Government will work with provinces, territories and municipalities to develop selective, smart regulation where appropriate?[222]

In the section called "Meeting our Targets," the government promises to "regularly assess progress and look at new opportunities."[223] That's the kind of detail one needs for a draft plan for a lemonade stand, or a garage sale. But for the most far-reaching treaty Canada has signed since free trade?

A plan says where the money comes from, and where it goes to. Forty-eight pages of vague ideas, jotted down in point form is not a plan.

In the rare instance where the government does mention a specific program, it only raises more questions than it answers. On page 36, the plan mentions "turn thermostat down at night, lower hot water temperature, fill clothes dryer, etc." Is that a suggestion for Canadians? Or will that become the law?

It is not a plan. A plan says who does what, when they do it, and who pays. A plan says where the money comes from, and where it goes to. Forty eight pages of vague ideas, jotted down in point form is not a plan.

Perhaps that is the whole point of the exercise. Because any plan that would truly meet the Kyoto requirements—cutting back on our energy use by a third—would be so shocking that Canadians would instantly and nearly unanimously revolt. We know the only plans that could take our energy-intensive economy

---

222 Government of Canada, p. 21.

223 Government of Canada, p. 22.

down by 30 per cent would need "high price shocks"[224] in the words of a government analyst. Kyoto can't be achieved by turning down the thermostat and putting on a sweater. There are two possibilities here, and they are both highly unappealing. Either our Environment Minister and his massive staff is utterly lazy, sloppy and unprofessional—for that is the picture painted by his draft plan—or, the Department is inhabited by industrious, detail-oriented technocrats, who have crafted a comprehensive Kyoto plan, but are waiting for Parliament to vote on the plan before revealing it.

Anderson's plan went over like a lead balloon. Pro-Kyoto lobbyists complained that the plan was too sketchy—they wanted tougher action, quicker. Industry and the provinces have similar remarks—the plan was a vague list of objectives, with no specifics—but their prescription was to slow down. Anderson started to get testy, a character trait that emerges when he gets into political trouble.

Nancy Hughes-Anthony, the president of the Canadian Chamber of Commerce had criticized the plan— an uncharacteristically bold move for a Canadian business leader. Anderson lost it: He dashed off a bitter letter to Hughes-Anthony and leaked it to the press, accusing her of bad faith, and spreading "inaccurate and misleading"[225] information—quite a charge, coming from the minister who hid economic impact assessments from his own cabinet colleagues.

---

224 Mark Jaccard, "Costing Greenhouse Gas Abatement," *Isuma*, Winter 2001.

225 Kate Jaimet, "Celebrities, executives fight to be heard," *Calgary Herald*, November 6, 2002, p. A11.

Anderson called Hughes-Anthony a liar, implying she really didn't care about finding a workable environmental policy:

> You say these things, but, at the same time, you are doing what you can to undermine the very consensus you claim to want.

This call for consensus, from the minister who told CBC radio that "a single province should not be able to prevent action by this country to combat greenhouse emissions."[226]

But the most hypocritical attack on Hughes-Anthony was Anderson's charge that

> the approach you support does not have targets. That's not a plan at all—a 'plan' is a strategy that will lead us to a particular objective.[227]

This, from the minister whose 4,000 employees, toiling for five years, could not himself muster better than a point-form "draft plan" of grade-school quality.

At least Anderson didn't call his opponent a caveman, like his Ontario provincial Liberal counterpart sometimes does. Jim Bradley, marshalling the best of his arguments, said:

> Whatever success that Mr. Klein has had over the years, he's always been known as an environmental Neanderthal.[228]

It's easy to see why Anderson and his friends are so testy. For five years they've wrung the public relations ben-

---

[226] David Anderson, *CBC Radio*, May 15, 2002.

[227] Kate Jaimet, "Celebrities, executives fight to be heard," *Calgary Herald*, November 6, 2002, p. A11.

[228] "Ontario critic paints Klein as a 'Neanderthal'," *Calgary Herald*, October 17, 2002 p. A5.

efits out of signing Kyoto, portraying themselves as keepers of the environment. They've boasted about Kyoto in two successive Red Book campaign platforms. They've issued countless self-congratulatory press releases about the treaty—and now people are starting to ask difficult questions about how it will all be achieved, without shutting down the economy.

With Anderson's anger has come desperation. His draft plan concedes that Canada cannot likely reduce our emissions to meet Kyoto standards, and that we will have to spend billions of dollars each year buying the "right" to burn fuel from countries such as Russia and the Ukraine. But even that math doesn't add up to Kyoto's targets. So Anderson thought he'd add his own wrinkle to Kyoto: Canada would simply not count any emissions that come from the energy we export to the United States, which would reduce our Kyoto emissions reduction obligation by 70 megatonnes a year.

Measuring carbon dioxide from every car, factory and cow in the country is a fanciful enough project as it is; who would notice or care if Canada simply didn't declare its energy export emissions?

Measuring carbon dioxide from every car, factory and cow in the country is a fanciful enough project as it is; who would notice or care if Canada simply did not declare its energy export emissions as part of its totals?

NO EXEMPTIONS FOR CANADA

The Europeans, that's who. "We are opposed to that particular proposal because it would upset the whole Kyoto

177

Protocol,"[229] says Margot Wallstrom, the European Union's Environment Commissioner. Anderson's proposal is just plain cheating, she says.

Philippe Musquar, the European Union Commissioner to Canada, is just as firm: "The commitments are there and they are not open for renegotiation," he says.[230]

It's not so much that Europe is concerned about reducing global emissions—after all, many European countries do not have to reduce their emissions at all under Kyoto and some, such as Portugal, are allowed double-digit emissions increases. What Europe was really concerned about was defenestrating Canada's energy economy, and forcing Canada to buy imaginary credits.

Anderson's accounting trick wasn't being accepted. Canada had signed the Kyoto Protocol, and Article 20 of the Protocol says that any changes need agreement by 75 per cent of the world's countries. Anderson says:

> We find it a little strange that the Europeans, for example, do not accept that this trade in clean energy that supplants dirtier fuels should not be encouraged in the Kyoto Protocol.[231]

But fair is fair, after all—Canada did sign the Kyoto Protocol as it was written, and crowed about that fact for five unrelenting years. "We just feel it bizarre," said Anderson.

That doesn't quite inspire confidence: We signed a treaty whose terms our minister finds bizarre.

---

[229] Margot Wallstrom, *The National*, CBC, April 16, 2002.

[230] Philippe Musquare, *The National*, CBC, September 5, 2002.

[231] David Anderson, *CBC Radio*, May 18, 2002.

CHAPTER EIGHTEEN

Template for Kyoto: The National Energy Program

Canadians have seen a Kyoto-style law before: the National Energy Program, a bundle of Canadian energy laws, in force from 1981 to 1986, designed to nationalize the energy industry, artificially fix the price of oil, subsidize certain high-risk exploration, and, most importantly, raise tens of billions of dollars in energy taxes for Ottawa. Ironically, one of the official purposes of the NEP was to increase the development of oil and gas in Canada—precisely the opposite of today's Kyoto rationale. And from 1982 to 1984, the Energy Minister in charge of enforcing the NEP was none other than Jean Chrétien.

HOW HISTORY IS BEING REPEATED

The story of the NEP illuminates the Kyoto debate for many reasons. In 1980, Pierre Trudeau, who had lost an election to the Joe Clark Tories the year before, was swept back into office, much to his own surprise. He knew that, in all likelihood, the 1980 election would be his last, and so he treated his last term as a bonus—unexpected, and unfettered by practical concerns like re-election. It was in this final term that Trudeau unveiled his grandest schemes, such as repatriating the Constitution from England, and drafting the Charter of Rights and Freedoms. The National Energy

Program was another such project—more than just another law or policy, it was to form Trudeau's grand legacy.

Jean Chrétien, too, is in his bonus term. He has already announced his resignation; he knows he will not be Prime Minister past the spring of 2004, if he can hold off Paul Martin's courtiers even that long. Like Trudeau, he can implement policies without regard for the political or economic consequences. And, like Trudeau, he has one last chance at leaving an indelible mark, a true signature on the country. He was one of Trudeau's closest ministers. He saw how it was done. And now he wants to do it himself. Implementing the Kyoto Protocol is Chrétien's plan to elevate himself from a workmanlike politician to a global statesman—and, if the man is permitted to dream, to perhaps inveigle his way into a new political career, as Secretary-General of the United Nations, once Kofi Annan retires.

> **Implementing the Kyoto Protocol is Chrétien's plan to elevate himself from a workmanlike politician to a global statesman.**

Besides the similarities in political motivation, there are many other ways that Kyoto mirrors the NEP. Like Kyoto, the NEP was predicated on economic predictions and guesswork that turned out to be spectacularly wrong. Like Kyoto, the NEP ended up driving energy production out of Canada, and into the United States. Like Kyoto, the NEP exacerbated regional tensions within Canada, and inflamed the embers of Western separatism—a phenomenon that is appearing again today in the shadow of Kyoto. And although Alberta was at the center of the NEP bulls-eye in the 1980s, Ontario and other provinces were sideswiped by massive job losses in the process, just as they will be with Kyoto.

In many cases, the same people who fought the NEP battles of the 1980s are fighting the Kyoto battles of the 2000s. Chrétien himself was the minister in charge of the NEP for two years. Peter Elzinga, an Alberta MP at the time and vocal critic of the NEP, is now the chief of staff to Premier Ralph Klein, quarterbacking Alberta's response.

Perrin Beatty, was another Tory MP who articulated the case against the NEP—from an Ontario perspective. Today he is the President of the Canadian Manufacturers and Exporters association, one of the leading business coalitions fighting Kyoto.

Another similarity between Kyoto and the NEP is the plethora of bureaucratic offices and programs that sprang up to manage the massive government intrusion into the economy. Back in the days of the NEP, there was a veritable alphabet soup: CHIP, COOP, COSC, IORT, NORP, PGRT, PIP, SOOP, TAP, and the unfortunately named PLOP.[232] Some were taxes, some were spending programs, but each one of them came with empire-building bureaucrats.

Similarly, Kyotocrats have created an industry unto themselves in Canada, with each province now having a team of bureaucrats assigned to the program, and hundreds of millions of dollars are earmarked each year by Canada's various political jurisdictions to be ladled out for Kyoto projects.

Unfortunately, the main similarity between the NEP and Kyoto is the massive job losses and economic recession that the NEP caused, and that Kyoto will cause.

The NEP was more focused than Kyoto is; where Kyoto will directly hit factories and car-owners in Ontario and

---

[232] As described by Paul Gagnon, *Hansard*, April 1, 1985.

Quebec, the NEP was targeted at Alberta, with collateral damage accruing to other Canadians.

A quick glance at the parliamentary debates during the NEP show a remarkable similarity to today's Kyoto debates. The economic losses back then were almost as staggering as those foreseen for Kyoto. Nearly four years into the program, Don Mazankowski noted:

> Today there are 378,000 people unemployed in Alberta and British Columbia. It is the highest number of people unemployed since 1946.[233]

The NEP targeted the oil patch, but it hit other industries too—such as the real estate sector. Calgary's office vacancy rate hit 21 per cent, rental accommodation vacancies touched 15 per cent. Jim Hawkes, an NEP opponent, said:

> When I read the National Energy Program, I stood in this House and said that Canadians would lose 300,000 jobs.
>
> I was wrong, Mr. Speaker; four years later 514,000 jobs had been lost, most of which are traceable to the disaster called the National Energy Program.[234]

As they are already starting to do in anticipation of Kyoto, investors simply took their money out of the country, to avoid the NEP. "Eighteen to twenty-two billion dollars of Canadian capital left Canada,"[235] Harvie Andre told Parliament in 1985, as the Tories began to dismantle the program.

---

[233] Don Mazankowski, *Hansard*, June 8, 1984.

[234] Jim Hawkes, *Hansard*, February 6, 1984.

[235] Harvey Andre, *Hansard*, September 25, 1985.

Industry, opposition parties, and the Western provinces all warned that economic chaos would be the result of such a centrally-planned intervention in the economy. But in April 1981, the government was still gritting its teeth in a smile, hoping that all of their rosy economic models would pay off. In response to a question about mounting job losses in Alberta and Ontario, Allan MacEachen, the Finance Minister, promised:

In April 1981, the government was still gritting its teeth in a smile, hoping that all of their rosy economic models would pay off.

> The honourable member ought to know that the rate of growth in western Canada for 1981 will be very strong indeed, stronger than most parts of the country.[236]

But it wasn't. In 1982, the Petroleum Resources Communication Foundation reported the devastation that set in after just one year of NEP.

> More than 200 drilling rigs moved to areas outside of Canada. Geophysical activity is down 45 per cent. Industry exploratory budgets are down 40 per cent. The decline in exploration activity has a significant impact on Canadian oil reserves. Remaining reserves at year end were down to pre-1962 levels. Cash available for reinvestment has been reduced 20-25 per cent; current taxes from the industry rose 75 per cent and interest payments on debt are up 100 per cent.

> Alsands, Cold Lake and expansion plans for the Suncor and Syncrude plants have been cancelled. Twenty thousand

---

[236] Allan MacEachen, *Hansard*, April 7, 1981.

jobs have been lost primarily in the drilling and service sectors of the industry. Hiring freezes have been adopted by many companies.[237]

Some of those same companies are still around today, opposing Kyoto with an unhappy premonition, a feeling of déjà vu. Many other companies don't have that problem—they didn't survive the first go-round.

Oil companies were targeted. Thousands of other companies—from auto dealerships to restaurants—depended on the continued employment of people working in the oil industry. Doug Roche noted, after just one year of NEP:

> The service sector in Alberta faces a 30 per cent drop in business, and bankruptcies are up 300 per cent over last year.[238]

THE NEP HIT OTHER REGIONS TOO

Of course the National Energy Program hit Alberta the hardest, with British Columbia and Saskatchewan close behind. Like the NEP, Kyoto only focuses on carbon-based fuels that are plentiful in the West, exempting Quebec's hydroelectric power and Ontario's nuclear plants. But in an integrated economy such as Canada's, smacking down one region doesn't always help another. For while oil workers were the direct victims of the NEP, those oil workers drove trucks made in Ontario, used heavy machinery made in Ontario, and had mortgages owing to banks in Ontario.

---

[237] Petroleum Resources Communication Foundation 1982, as quoted by Don Mazankowski, *Hansard*, May 14, 1985.

[238] Douglas Roche, *Hansard*, June 8, 1981.

According to Ontario's Department of Energy, "the NEP cost Ontario 90,000 jobs and was responsible for price hikes amounting to 33 per cent of all inflation" in the early 1980s.[239] As Peter Elzinga noted in the House of Commons at the time, "unemployment stalks Ontario industry which is being deprived of machinery and equipment orders" because of the Alberta slowdown.[240]

William Jarvis, an MP from Perth, Ontario, had this lament for the NEP:

> I am told, and I accept it, that the largest industrial customer of trucking is the petroleum industry. What do they make in these small plants in Stratford? They make brake cables; they make upholstery; they make oil filters; they make fan belts. These are the places that are laying off their employees.

Today's MP from Perth should be concerned about Kyoto's impact on Alberta, too. But Kyoto is coming for anyone in Ontario who consumes energy—not just people in Alberta who produce it. Jarvis continued:

> I wish [the Prime Minister] would visit Stratford or Woodstock or St. Thomas and the multitude of small Canadian cities in Ontario and Quebec. The unemployment lines there are a direct result of the National Energy Policy...[241]

> If one tar-sands plant went ahead, I think we would have the potential for 300 jobs in one plant in the city of Stratford for welders, boil makers, tool and dye makers,

---

[239] Jim Edwards, *Hansard*, November 13, 1984.

[240] Peter Elzinga, *Hansard*, June 16, 1981.

[241] William Jarvis, *Hansard*, April 13, 1981.

and machinists and as well, there would be all the feeding plants that would supply that one industry.

Kyoto hasn't even been implemented yet, but oil sands investors have announced their intentions to scale down development because of Kyoto risks.

And Perrin Beatty, then the Member of Parliament for Wellington-Dufferin-Simcoe, said:

> I do not think my constituents will be fooled into believing that slowdowns in oil exploration and development in western Canada will not have a very serious effect upon their jobs right here in the heartland of Canada, because it is Ontario which benefits most from the manufacturing which is required to supply the oil industry, and a slowdown in the industry affects jobs right here in the industrial heartland of Canada.[242]

In the face of this withering proof of government failure, Jean Chrétien refused to blink. In 1983, when the full devastation of the NEP was readily known, an opposition MP from Calgary asked Chrétien if he would even acknowledge "the degree of the devastation" caused by the NEP. Chrétien's reply:

> I do not know if that is a very appropriate question. I could go on and explain all the policies, the advantages, and the convenience of every policy.

The more things change, the more they stay the same. When Chrétien's response prompted jeers, he added:

> At this time in western Canada I am having very good relations with the Government of Alberta. When I meet representatives of the industry, they receive me very well.

---

[242] Perrin Beatty, *Hansard*, November 25, 1980.

In fact in Calgary the other day, 1,650 people from the Chamber of Commerce came to hear me. It is certainly not a very hostile climate.[243]

Perhaps that's how if felt from up on the stage; but Calgary has not elected a Liberal MP in nearly 35 years.

A NEW SEPARATIST THREAT IN THE WEST

Marc Lalonde, the inventor of the NEP, was also wilfully blind to the strain that his plans were putting on the Western bonds of Canadian nationalism. Perhaps Lalonde and Chrétien were too focused on appeasing separatism in their own province to notice how they were fostering the same disenchantment out West. Lalonde told Parliament in April 1980:

> Energy is an obvious example of the benefits that Quebec derives from its participation in the Canadian federation...
>
> It demonstrates also how a dynamic national energy policy makes it possible for a region to develop its own positive resources in its own way, while recognizing its responsibilities to the rest of Canada and sharing the wealth of other regions. Canadians must unite and state positively their need for a national energy policy; we have to wonder what our separatists have to offer.

Lalonde was clearly speaking about Quebec separatists, who had called a referendum for May 20 of that year. Lalonde knew his role in the referendum—make energy an issue.

> Some PQ ministers even go so far as to say that Quebeckers should pay world prices for their oil. Are they

---

[243] Jean Chrétien, *Hansard*, June 7, 1983.

really aware of what they are saying? If it did pay world prices, Quebec would immediately, and I insist immediately, have to pay $3.8-billion more a year for its oil.[244]

Nearly 60 per cent of Quebeckers voted against separation; how much of that is attributable to Lalonde's overt promises of subsidized energy is unknown. But while Lalonde, Chrétien and Trudeau were busy slaying one separatist dragon in Quebec, they had awakened another in the West.

In October 1980, when the NEP was still being cobbled together, 28 per cent of Western Canadians agreed with that separatist sentiment.

Later that year, the Canada West Foundation started tracking public opinion to survey voters to see if they agreed with the statement: "Western Canadians get so few benefits from being part of Canada that they might as well go it on their own." In October 1980, when the NEP was still being cobbled together, 28 per cent[245] of Western Canadians agreed with that separatist sentiment—a number very similar to an October 2002 survey that put Alberta separatism on the eve of Kyoto at 23 per cent in Calgary, 20 per cent province-wide.[246]

By March 1981, Western separatism had bloomed to 36 per cent; by June it was at a full 49 per cent in Alberta—or exactly as high as Quebec separatism was in that province's 1995 referendum on sovereignty.

---

244 Marc Lalonde, *Hansard*, April 16, 1980.

245 As cited by Douglas Roche, *Hansard*, June 8, 1981.

246 Bill Kaufmann, "Separation Anxiety," *Calgary Sun*, October 28, 2002, p. 4.

Less than a year into the NEP, Tory MP Peter Elzinga summed it up thusly:

> The National Energy Program after seven months has managed to cripple the Canadian exploration industry and to drive it out of the country, to increase Canadian oil consumption, to disrupt the supply of existing oil, to ship millions upon millions of dollars overseas, to jeopardize relations with the Americans, to expose us far more to dependence on Arab oil, to halt development of the tar sands, to throw federal-provincial relations into chaos bordering on legal civil war, and to find no oil. All that in seven months!

INVESTMENT IN THE OIL SANDS STALLS

Just like the NEP's Marc Lalonde, Kyoto's David Anderson keeps insisting that the economy will survive his meddling—though studies by Anderson's own department show otherwise. Elzinga commented on the worthlessness of such promises twenty years ago:

> The reassurances of the federal minister of energy that everything would return to normal have turned out to be dead wrong...he had no idea whatever of the damage he was about to wreak upon his country. It was a case of too much power exercised in both arrogance and ignorance with calamitous consequence to the industry and the nation whose ill fortune it was to have been left in his hands.[247]

Can the same not be said about Anderson, willfully blind to his own economic studies, and about Chrétien, thinking only of his retirement legacy?

When critics of the NEP warned that economic calamity was coming, they were unheeded by a government that was

---

[247] Peter Elzinga, *Hansard*, June 16, 1981.

so stubbornly committed to its grand economic theories and schemes that it would hear no dissent. That same unhappy pattern has repeated itself with Kyoto. When Jean Chrétien came to Calgary to lay down the law to the oil patch—just as he did twenty years ago—he did not allay fears, he confirmed them. He told oil men:

When Jean Chrétien came to Calgary to lay down the law to the oil patch—just as he did twenty years ago—he did not allay fears, he confirmed them.

No business in a market economy operates in a completely risk free environment. I recognize that our Kyoto obligations add to the uncertainty you face. Our job is to work with you to minimize that uncertainty...

That we will do. We will give assurances as to how much cost and risk each sector of society will be asked to bear.[248]

Hardly an inspirational message of hope—the only assurances the Prime Minister was giving was that, indeed, there would be cost and risk. The distribution of that pain between the provinces and industries was all that remained open for negotiation. That the pain was indeed coming was a fait accompli.

TrueNorth Energy, a company with a multi-billion dollar investment in the oil patch, didn't need to be told twice. After the Prime Minister's speech, it announced it would freeze three-quarters of its planned spending on a $3.3-billion oil sands project. The job losses have already begun—putting a lie to the government's economic fantasy scenario.

---

[248] Jean Chrétien, speech at the Liberal Party's Calgary Leader's Dinner, September 18, 2002.

David Anderson, the Environment Minister, was apoplectic. He slammed TrueNorth in the media, claiming the company's rational and timing made him "skeptical" about their motives. "They need better scriptwriters...this is pretty clumsy stuff," he said.[249]

TrueNorth's "script," however, was all too familiar—it was the only movie playing in Alberta in the 1980s. David Park, TrueNorth's president, was the opposite of the hot and irate Environment Minister. He said:

> I am not confident that [Chrétien] can achieve both his oil sands objectives and his Kyoto objectives at the same time...The policies are at odds with each other.

With $3.3-billion on the line, TrueNorth decided not to gamble on a legacy-hunting Prime Minister who—of all the politicians in the country—was actually the same man who enforced the NEP.

TrueNorth isn't the only company ratcheting down spending and employment plans. Husky Energy Inc. has also scaled back its oil sands plans. And in November 2002, Canadian Natural Resources Limited announced that it had put $100-million in capital spending on ice. Steve Laut, CNRL's Vice President of Operations, said:

> Essentially what we have done here is to slow down...until we have clarification of what will happen with Kyoto...We need to know that before we spend more money."[250]

---

[249] "It's started: Oil sands delay represents first ill effects of Kyoto Protocol on Alberta," *Calgary Herald*, September 22, 2002 p. A12.

[250] Mike Leschart, "CNRL Says Horizon Delay Due To Kyoto Uncertainty," *Daily Oil Bulletin*, November 6, 2002, p. 3.

Perhaps Environment Minister Anderson would write this off as just the same old anti-Liberal "script." But CNRL's board of directors is gold-plated Liberal[251]— including Murray Edwards, arguably the highest profile Liberal in Calgary's oil patch, and Jim Palmer, the city's top Liberal fundraiser for Paul Martin's leadership campaign.

Dr. Michael Percy, the former Finance Critic for the Alberta Liberal Opposition, has also fired back at Kyoto. "We will see a decline in standards of living due to a decrease in productivity," he said. Kyoto is an "environmental trade barrier."[252]

Anderson's emotional outburst may have simply been one of embarrassment. That spring, when he had unveiled several Kyoto options, he boasted on national radio that not a single job would be lost because of his plans. He said cheerfully:

> Don't forget, nothing proposed in any of these options…would reduce employment by one person at the current time, or reduce the GDP by one dollar.[253]

It seems that Anderson's script was the one needing some editing.

---

251 *Annual Report 2001*, Canadian Natural Resources Limited, p. 74.

252 Scott Hamilton, "Brain drain feared if Kyoto's ratified," *Calgary Sun*, November 9, 2002.

253 David Anderson, *CBC Radio*, May 15, 2002.

CHAPTER NINETEEN

Will the Federal Environment Minister Blink?

Federal Environment Minister David Anderson is clearly a Kyoto believer—like David Suzuki, his attachment to the treaty is emotional, almost religious. He doesn't just support it, he truly believes in it. But *Edmonton Journal* and *National Post* columnist Lorne Gunter, one of Canada's earliest and best-informed Kyoto critics, says that even the most ideological Liberal might put political survival ahead ideological purity. Gunter points out that, already, Anderson is looking for face-saving ways to get out of gutting Canada's economy, which would be a sure-fire election loser. That's why Anderson is so adamant about getting credit for clean energy exports, even though the Protocol doesn't allow for it. And that's why Canada's draft plan is banking on spending billions of dollars to buy emissions credits from foreign countries, in lieu of shutting down Canadian industry. Commenting on Anderson's draft plan, Gunter said:

> We saw what little they'd like to get away with. That implementation strategy boiled down to, basically: Wear a sweater! Ride the bus!
>
> We will see lots more turn-your-thermostats-down,

cross-country-ski-to-work public service advertising exhorting us to be more like the Norwegians.[254]

Besides hiding from the public the true degree of deindustrialization inherent in Kyoto, Gunter predicts the Liberals will find ways to channel Kyoto dollars towards their favourite corporate friends, in the name of investing in green technology.

> Liberal darlings such as Ballard Power Systems Inc. will be huge winners, because Ottawa hopes some sort of Philosopher's Stone can be found that will enable us to achieve our Kyoto reductions by magic—by discovery or invention of a magic wand that can be waved over our economy that both preserves our affluence and enables us to meet our Kyoto commitments.

The fact that Ballard made a five-figure donation to the Liberal party last year[255] certainly doesn't hurt that hypothesis. Gunter said:

> We'll see billions going to dirty, non-Kyoto economies such as Russia's, China's and India's for cleaner kilns, turbines, etc. so we can claim "credits."

Anything to buy our way out of meeting impossible reductions at home.

If that's all the Kyoto implementation turns out to be—a massive new program of foreign aid, in the ways carbon traders like Aldyen Donnelly predict—then Kyoto will turn out to be nothing more than a tax hike. It will hobble our overtaxed economy even more than it already is, but it won't directly stop our use of energy.

---

254 Lorne Gunter, personal interview, November 12, 2002.

255 Elections Canada, *Political Parties' Financial Reports*, "Statement of Contributions Received, 2001-Liberal Party of Canada," Ottawa, 2002.

That could be the Liberal approach to implementation—take a lot of friendly environmental publicity by ratifying the deal, but in the end, just buy forgiveness for not meeting the targets. The problem with that, however, is that by ratifying Kyoto, the government of Canada is transforming that unworkable treaty into binding Canadian law—and that is a tempting target for environmentalists lawyers. Says Gunter:

> Greens are already schooling up to sue the feds (and presumably the provinces) if they fail to meet Kyoto's legally binding targets. One of the principal reasons Japan merely "accepted" the accord rather than implementing it was to avoid making it legally binding.

Even the country whose city is the namesake to the Kyoto Protocol is afraid of it—and, according to Gunter, we have even more reason to fear than they do.

> Crusading judges, who do not have to face voters over Kyoto's human costs, could well prove an easier touch for environmentalists than politicians. Thus if we ratify and make Kyoto legally binding, we may find the courts and the greens forcing us into implementation, even if the politicians chicken out.

That could be the Liberal approach to implementation—take a lot of friendly environmental publicity by ratifying the deal, but in the end, just buy forgiveness for not meeting the targets.

The Report magazine publisher Ted Byfield, another Kyoto critic, says that if the federal government raids Alberta's resource sector, it would be Ottawa that abandons the terms of Confederation, not the other way around. "It would in fact be an act of separatism conducted from the federal level,"[256] says Byfield. "Any Ottawa government that sought to override provincial control of resources would be violating an absolute principle of the contract that made Canada"—and the terms of the Canadian contract would be broken.

Charles Frank, the business editor of the *Calgary Herald* and a well-regarded columnist with *Business in Calgary* magazine, says Kyoto has created "a widespread feeling of frustration" in the West. He claims:

> Albertans have no palpable desire to separate a la Quebec.... And even during the height of the heinous NEP, when there was every reason to contemplate an exit strategy or our own, we held firm.

But Frank ends his plaintive call for understanding with a veiled threat. Opposing Kyoto and its devastating effects on the oil patch "doesn't make us separatists," he says. "Yet."[257]

For a pillar of Calgary's establishment—a leading business columnist, who has spent years cultivating contacts and relationships in the industry—to concede that separatism may yet flourish is an astounding fact. Charles Frank is no wild-eyed Western rights crusader; he's a chronicler of Calgary business. But the frustration he sees is evidently enough to make even him hint about radical anti-Kyoto strategies.

According to political watchers like Lorne Gunter, Albertans are already sore about how the province has been

---

256 Ted Byfield, "Kyoto an Act of Independence," *Edmonton Sun*, September 8, 2002.

257 Charles Frank, "No separatists here! (Yet)," *Business in Calgary*, November 2002, p. 52.

treated by Chrétien, ranging from gun control, to the monopolistic Canadian Wheat Board, to Alberta being Chrétien's favourite whipping boy on the health care issue. Kyoto could be the last straw. Alberta alienation— always latent—could turn into "a full-blown separatist movement.... It may never succeed, but it could be a factor quickly."[258]

Kyoto could be the last straw. Alberta alienation— always latent— could turn into "a full-blown" separatist movement.

RECENT PUBLIC OPINION

Ten years ago, Canadians were faced with another complicated subject: the Charlottetown Accord. It wasn't a foreign treaty, but rather a complex amendment to Canada's Constitution. Like Kyoto, however, it was overwhelmingly supported by the media and other opinion leaders. And not only did it have the full backing of the federal government, but most of the provinces, too.

When the Charlottetown Accord was first released, public opinion polls showed it was exceedingly popular until people started to actually read the thing. The more they learned, the more questions they had. And, over the course of several months, public opinion reversed itself. By the time Canadians voted on the subject in a referendum, it was rejected, nearly two to one.

The lesson from the Charlottetown Accord is that information is the key to fighting bad public policy. The more people knew about Charlottetown, the more they read, the more they heard about it on talk radio, the more

[258] Lorne Gunter, personal interview, November 12, 2002.

they disliked it, or at least had serious questions. The Kyoto treaty is even more complex than Charlottetown, because it is based on abstruse and conflicting science and economics. As Chris Stockwell, Ontario's Environment Minister, said, if you ask people "What do you think of the Kyoto Accord," they would "probably think you're talking about a car."[259] Still, public education is starting to turn things around.

In a major poll done by JMCK Polling, more than 1,000 Albertans were asked whether they supported the treaty. Just 24 per cent did, with 57 per cent opposing it.

For example, a 1,000-person public opinion poll commissioned by the Sun Media newspapers shows that fully 55 per cent of Canadians want ratification of Kyoto to be put on hold—at least until "there is a better understanding of its impact on the economy."[260] Importantly, 57 per cent of Ontarians want the brakes put on, too—an encouraging sign that Canada's biggest province understands that Kyoto is not just a problem for Alberta's oil patch.

That's not to say that Alberta isn't especially sensitive to Kyoto. In a major poll done by JMCK Polling,[261] more than 1,000 Albertans were asked whether they supported the treaty. Just 24 per cent did, with 57 per cent opposing it, and another 12 per cent saying they needed more information.

---

259 April Lindgren, "Ontarians think accord a car: minister," *Calgary Herald*, October 22, 2002, p. A14.

260 Bill Rodgers, "Kyoto support cools off," *Calgary Sun*, November 7, 2002.

261 *Alberta Omnibus Poll*, November, 2002, JMCK Polling.

But it was the next question that should seize the attention of any Canadian who wants to avoid a Western repeat of the Quebec separation saga:

If the federal government ratifies Kyoto against the wishes of the Alberta government, what do you think Alberta should do?

Forty four per cent of Albertans said "there's nothing we can do"—a statistic that presumably includes the 24 per cent of Albertans who want the treaty. But a larger number—47 per cent—said "Albertans should begin to explore other options such as independence from Canada." And yet another 9 per cent said "Alberta should seek to join the United States."

But a larger number—47 per cent—said "Albertans should begin to explore other options such as independence from Canada."

A full majority of Albertans say they would want to leave the country—either to go it alone, or to join the U.S. That is a higher number than voted for separation in Quebec in either the 1980 or 1995 Referendums—a statistic that is even more powerful, considering the absence of a separatist party fomenting such sentiment. Ordinary Albertans have already made up their minds, without a Western Parti Quebecois stoking them up: If Kyoto comes in, Albertans want out.

CHAPTER TWENTY

The Clean Energy Act

There is no silver bullet that can kill Kyoto—if there was, it would have already been shot by a provincial government panicked about job losses, or an industry in Kyoto's crosshairs. And, given the concentration of power in the Prime Minister's office, there are some threats that are simply unstoppable, if the occupant of that office—be he Chrétien or Martin—simply wants to do it.

Like the National Energy Program of the 1980's, the Kyoto Accord will likely be a bundle of laws and regulations that all fall under the same media nickname, some of which are more dangerous than others. Much of Kyoto is simply government bumph, meaningless public relations to give the appearance of activity. For Kyoto fighters, those elements of Kyoto implementation will be little more than a political irritant, and waste of money in the hundred-million dollar range—vapid television and newspaper ads, and bumper-sticker-style sloganeering. Strategically, this politically correct huffing and puffing can actually turn into a good thing for Kyoto fighters— because if the truly dangerous elements of Kyoto are successfully stymied, the remaining propaganda of achievement might be enough to meet the public opinion standard of "action" without devastating the economy.

But other parts of Kyoto—the job-destroying, investment-killing parts, the active ingredients—must be fought. And some of them can be.

Taxes on energy consumers—like the mooted new tax on sport utility vehicles, or the inevitable thirty- or forty-cent hike in gasoline taxes—are certainly active ingredients in the Kyoto implementation plan. But they are not the essence of Kyoto; they are not what makes Kyoto unique or different. Gasoline taxes existed before the Kyoto environmental rationale was invented; Kyoto is simply a pretext upon which to increase an already lucrative source of revenue for Ottawa's thirsty coffers. An SUV tax is indeed new—and punitive, and smacks of class envy—but it, too, is not the heart of Kyoto.

> But other parts of Kyoto—the job-destroying, investment-killing parts, the active ingredients—must be fought. And some of them can be.

The central pillar of Kyoto is the reduction in the production and use of carbon-based fuels, such as oil and gas, and it is there that Kyoto will succeed or fail. Everything else that will appear in Ottawa's Kyoto plan is just a tax grab or a regulation along for the ride.

It is Kyoto's attack on carbon-based fuels that will demolish the economy of Alberta, NEP-style, and do significant damage to other provinces that benefit from oil, gas and coal, including British Columbia, Saskatchewan, and, lately, Nova Scotia and Newfoundland.

The authority of the federal government to make decisions about the production of these fuels was one of the most powerful elements of the NEP, a fact not lost on then-Premier of Alberta Peter Lougheed. Lougheed used that power as a bargaining chip with Pierre Trudeau in the negotiations to repatriate the Canadian Constitution from the United Kingdom. In return for Lougheed's signature to the Constitution Act, 1982, Lougheed had a new provision added, giving provinces the power to manage non-renewable resources.

It is Kyoto's attack on carbon-based fuels that will demolish the economy of Alberta, NEP-style.

Section 91 of the old British North America Act, enacted in 1867, outlined the federal government's areas of authority, ranging from the right to print money and run the post office to the right to sign foreign treaties. Section 92 outlined the provinces' rights, from the right to run schools and hospitals to the right to regulate matters of property and civil rights. Under the Constitution, anything that wasn't specifically given to the provinces, became Ottawa's turf, and so issues that were not contemplated by Queen Victoria's ministers—such as the energy wars of the 1970s and 1980s—fell to Ottawa by default. Lougheed's deal saw the addition of section 92A, more than a century later.

Section 92A came too late to stop the NEP. Two years after it was enacted, Trudeau's Liberals were defeated, and Brian Mulroney's Progressive Conservatives slowly began to dismantle the NEP—but not before raking in tens of billions of dollars more in taxes from it.

But section 92A is not too late to stop Kyoto, or at least to weaken it, delay it, rally a national counter-attack to it, and to begin to make it too politically expensive for the Liberals—especially a new Liberal leader—to pursue.

The language of 92A could not be more clear: "In each province, the legislature may exclusively make laws" in relation to a list of resource issues, including development, conservation and management of non-renewable natural resources and forestry resources in the province, including laws in relation to the rate of primary production therefrom.

Section 92A also gives provinces exclusive jurisdiction regarding

development, conservation and management of sites and facilities in the province for the generation and production of electrical energy.

Much of this electrical energy, throughout Canada, is generated through the burning of natural gas and coal, two Kyoto-targeted energy sources.

The key word here is "exclusively"—it means that only the provinces can pass a law on these matters. The federal government's Kyoto package can pass laws all around the subject matter of section 92A but it cannot touch the development of oil and gas.

Section 92A is like a shark cage for scuba divers. The sharks can swarm around the cage, growl at the diver inside the cage, and even bump up against the cage, but water inside the cage is the sole jurisdiction—exclusive jurisdiction, to use the words of the Constitution—of the diver inside.

And the best time to build a shark cage and get into it is before the sharks actually come.

WHY IT'S BETTER TO WRITE A PROVINCIAL LAW, THAN TO CHALLENGE A FEDERAL LAW

Some pundits suggest that the provinces sue the federal government, to get them to stop Kyoto in its tracks, to get an injunction against the entire treaty. But that won't work—section 132 of the Constitution Act, 1867, gives the federal government the sole right to enter into treaties. It's like the army, or postage stamps in that way: it's something that only Ottawa can do. No matter how foolish the treaty, it is Parliament's right to sign it—something that Canada has already done.

Suing to stop Canada from ratifying Kyoto is also out— while to the UN ratification is a higher level of agreement than just plain signing a treaty, it is still wholly within Ottawa's rights to do so. The main reason the UN made the distinction for Kyoto is that once all of the diplomats drafted and signed Kyoto back in 1997, they were allowed to take it back to their home countries for double-checking. When 55 per cent of countries representing 55 per cent of greenhouse gas emissions confirm their participation, the treaty kicks into effect.

Just because Ottawa has the sole constitutional right to negotiate, sign and ratify treaties, however, does not give it the power to implement treaties, if the treaties step on provincial toes. A foreign treaty cannot give the federal government any powers that our own Constitution does not grant.

A foreign treaty cannot give the federal government any powers that our own Constitution does not grant.

This is a point noted by Lorne Taylor, Alberta's Environment Minister.[262]

We own the resources, so how can Ottawa force an action on us that can really desperately damage us? …Constitutionally, we own our resources. Therefore, we need to defend Alberta's rights under the Constitution.

---

262 Shawn Ohler, "Minister pushes Kyoto lawsuit," *Edmonton Journal*, March 18, 2002, p. A1.

Predicting what the courts will do is a dangerous business—especially when Supreme Court judges are hand-picked by the Prime Minister. Five out of nine of today's Supreme Court judges were appointed by Jean Chrétien himself, and the Chief Justice was promoted to that position by Chrétien, too. Canada's Supreme Court is not corrupt—but they are political people. And, by definition, a majority of them are Chrétien's people. It is a dangerous place for provinces to go to sue Chrétien.

Michael Ritter, former Parliamentary Counsel to the Alberta Legislature, predicts "if this ever came to a court settled issue, the federal government would prevail."[263] That's not a certainty, of course. But every important provincial challenge in recent years—from gun control to jurisdiction over toxic substances—has been rebuffed by the Supreme Court, in favour of the feds. "What a laugh,"[264] says Ted Byfield, Alberta's conservative patriarch.

> Relying on the court to save the Alberta case amounts to a total capitulation. It signals Ottawa to take what it likes, do what it likes.

Suing the federal government to stop Kyoto isn't just legally risky; it is a public relations statement by whichever province that launches the suit. Given the media cheerleading on Kyoto, any province that would dare to oppose it—especially if it were Alberta or Ontario—would be quickly portrayed as an uncooperative, self-centred aberration. The optics of the federal government building something, and

---

[263] Michael Ritter, *CBC Radio*, September 3, 2002.

[264] Ted Byfield, "Kyoto an Act of Independence," *Edmonton Sun*, September 8, 2002.

then a province attacking it, naturally sets up Ottawa as a constructive force that wants to take steps to care for the environment, and the province as a recalcitrant, obstinate loophole-seeker. Things are already bad enough at the CBC and *The Toronto Star* for Ernie Eves and Ralph Klein.

To be sure, such a provincial lawsuit—even if it lost in the end—would likely delay Kyoto, and could serve as a forum to educate the public and the media about the scientific and economic flaws in the treaty. As Ritter, the province's former parliamentary lawyer, says, "Alberta can make it very, very ugly for Ottawa."[265]

DRAFTING NEW PROVINCIAL LAWS

For a province to fight Ottawa in the Supreme Court, it would be like a scuba diver going after the sharks. The unbounded ocean is the shark's natural habitat; it's fighting the sharks on their terms.

The last, best hope is to enact provincial laws of their own—first, before Ottawa enacts its implementation legislation for Kyoto.

Why not build something strong—like a steel shark cage—and let the sharks worry about going on the attack?

Alberta, Ontario and other provinces that want protection from Kyoto can't just sit idly by; but they can't likely sue in the superior courts, either. The last, best hope is to enact provincial laws of their own—first, before Ottawa enacts its implementation legislation for Kyoto, before the dozens of Kyoto taxes, regulations, and restrictions are put together. As David Anderson says, "the

---

[265] Michael Ritter, *CBC Radio*, September 3, 2002.

ratification issue is separate from the development of a plan."[266] The provinces must move first, to beat Ottawa to the punch—something that, given the laughably unprepared "draft plan" release in October 2002 by Anderson, won't be too difficult.

Section 92A can be the seed for the provincial laws to keep the Kyoto sharks out. Alberta could be the first to enact such a law, and other provinces concerned about a Kyoto-style attack on their energy or electricity industries could follow suit. Each provincial act could be slightly different, allowing for local emphases—Ontario's law would likely focus more on electricity generation, while Alberta's would focus on every aspect of energy production. These provincial laws would be enacted before the federal government enacted their Kyoto implementation laws and regulations, so that the provincial laws would take up the legislative space delineated by section 92A—building the shark cage before the sharks arrive.

Each province's section 92A laws would likely have a slightly varied motivation too. For example, Newfoundland and Nova Scotia's laws would emphasize the job-creation benefits of producing offshore oil; Ontario's might highlight the growing industrial and residential demands for energy, and the importance of avoiding power shortages and "brown-outs" in the Greater Toronto Area, like those experienced by other North American megalopolises, such as New York and Los Angeles.

Alberta's section 92A law would have all of these elements in it. Energy production means jobs in Alberta; it also

---

[266] David Anderson, press conference at the Halifax Environment and Natural Resources Minister meeting, October 29, 2002.

means feeding the energy needs of Alberta's booming population, the fastest-growing in the country. But Alberta has an additional rationale: Energy produced in Alberta is cleaner than energy produced almost anywhere else in the world. If indeed the ideological rationale behind Kyoto is to produce energy in the most efficient, environmentally-friendly manner possible, then every barrel of oil bought from clean Alberta is a barrel of oil that is not bought from environmentally apathetic Mexico. Alberta energy is also produced in the most socially ethical manner in the world. Every barrel of oil bought from free and democratic Alberta is a barrel of oil that is not bought from cruel dictatorships such as Saudi Arabia.

Canadian energy is not just important for the benefits it brings to Canada—jobs and energy self-sufficiency. It is important in that it provides the world community with a source of politically reliable, environmentally superior and ethically unimpeachable oil.

Restricting the production of Canadian energy will only serve to drive energy buyers to non-Kyoto countries. The world's thirst for energy will be quenched—will clean, ethical Canadians quench it? Or will other countries that do not share our values of democratic and environmental responsibility?

Canada as a whole is a clean energy country—our energy sources are cleaner than the U.S., and even cleaner than European countries that do not face the onerous Kyoto rationing that we do.

Half of the electricity in the U.S., for example, is generated from burning coal; more than 30 per cent of Europe's carbon dioxide emissions are from burning coal, too. Canada, on the other hand, generates only 7.5 per cent of our electrical energy from burning coal.[267] Kyoto's restrictions on Canada would not only devastate our country economically, they would drive energy production—including electrical production—out of clean Canada and into the U.S., where energy production is dirtier than it is here. Ironically, implementing Kyoto in Canada—especially to the energy sector—will result in a dirtier world.

Canada as a whole is a clean energy country—our energy sources are cleaner than the U.S., and even cleaner than European countries that do not face the onerous Kyoto rationing that we do.

That is Alberta's unique rationale for enacting a law under section 92A. Strictly speaking, no such lofty rationale is required—the Constitution gives the provinces the unfettered and exclusive right to pass laws about energy production, and that is legal grounds enough. But the economic and environmental foundations of such a law would trump Kyoto on idealistic grounds, too. And that's the advantage of proactively building a constructive law, rather than waiting for Ottawa's law and then litigating.

Provinces should enact laws to fill up the regulatory void. They should enact programs to generate momentum, set the precedent, put Ottawa on the defensive, and let the public know that the provinces aren't just negative critics—they have their own plans, too.

Let Ottawa sue the provinces—how would that go over in the court of public opinion? Would a new Liberal leader

---

[267] Canadian Manufacturers and Exporters, *Pain Without Gain: Canada and the Kyoto Protocol*, p. 8.

risk antagonizing millions of voters in a province that felt picked on? And let the provinces stake out their section 92A turf cleanly, so that any federal challenge would be on provincial ground.

By contrast, if a province tried to attack federal Kyoto implementation laws, Ottawa could argue that the main purpose of Kyoto is not to meddle with section 92A energy or electricity production and management, but for abstract environmental reasons. Whoever writes the first law, gets to choose what the debate will be about. If the provinces move first with their laws, the debate will be framed about provincial rights in general, and section 92A rights in particular. If Ottawa moves first, the debate will be over "the environment" and other ill-defined grey jurisdictional areas—giving the Supreme Court enough wiggle-room to side with Ottawa, as is their tendency.

Each concerned province should draft its own section 92A law. Here is what Alberta's could look like. It need not be long, or fancy. It just has to be strong, like a shark cage. The law would be formally written in the proper legal language of the legislature; but here are the essential elements, in plain English:

CLEAN ENERGY ACT

WHEREAS Alberta's energy industry is the most environmentally clean in the world, and continually improves its environmental standards;

WHEREAS Alberta's energy industry is the most ethically and socially responsible in the world, and continually improves its development and nurturing of its workforce and host communities at home and in other countries;

WHEREAS Alberta-based international energy companies serve to transfer and propagate Alberta's high environmental and social standards to parts of the world that benefit from that environmental and social leadership;

WHEREAS Alberta's share of the world's energy production displaces energy produced in less environmentally and socially responsible jurisdictions, and it is the responsibility of the Government of Alberta to encourage the production of environmentally clean and socially responsible energy, both for domestic use and export;

WHEREAS Alberta receives significant tax revenues and other economic benefits from the production of non-renewable natural resources and electrical energy, and maximizing that production is therefore essential to the well-being of the province;

WHEREAS section 92A of the Constitution Act, 1867 gives Alberta exclusive jurisdiction over the development, conservation and management of non-renewable natural resources in Alberta, including laws in relation to the rate of primary production;

AND WHEREAS section 92A of the Constitution Act, 1867 also gives Alberta exclusive jurisdiction over the development, conservation and management of sites and facilities in Alberta for the generation and production of electrical energy;

THEREFORE HER MAJESTY, by and with the advice and consent of the Legislative Assembly of Alberta, enacts as follows.

DEFINITIONS

1. *"Electrical plant"* is any business, facility or site that generates electrical power;

"Non-renewable energy plant" is any business, facility or site relating to the development, conservation or management of non-renewable energy;

"Annual production plan" is an annual plan submitted to the Department of Energy by any electrical plant or non-renewable power plant, describing development, production, conservation and management targets for each plant;

"Production permit" is a permit by the Government of Alberta approving an annual production plan;

"Cumulative annual production" is the cumulative annual amount of energy produced under all annual production plans.

SUBMISSION OF ANNUAL PRODUCTION PLANS

2. Each year, all electrical plants and non-renewable energy plants shall submit their annual production plans to the Minister of Energy.

3. Any electrical plant or non-renewable energy plant may submit a production plan amendment, at any time.

PUBLICATION OF CUMULATIVE ANNUAL PRODUCTION

4. Once a year, the Minister of Energy shall announce the cumulative annual production, which shall formally serve as a legally binding minimum level of production.

ISSUANCE OF PRODUCTION PERMITS

5. Subject to any other provincial statute or regulation, the Minister of Energy shall issue a permit to any electrical

plant or non-renewable energy plant approving annual production plans and amendments.

LEGAL DEFENCE

6. Should the validity of a production permit be infringed upon by the Government of Canada, the Government of Alberta shall provide a legal defence for the production permit, if requested by the affected permit holder.

ANNUAL REPORT

7. The Minister of Energy shall issue an annual public report. The annual report shall describe the state of environmental and social responsibility in the global energy market, and Alberta's position in that context.

It's not a poetic law. It sure isn't the Magna Carta. But it has one job, and one job only: To benefit Alberta by ensuring that Alberta's resources are produced in the most economically and environmentally sustainable manner, and to benefit the world by producing resources in an environmentally advantageous manner. And, should the law ever be challenged in court, it should be upheld as wholly within section 92A.

The preamble of the Clean Energy Act is just as long as the law itself. That's important, both from a court of law and court of public opinion point of view. In the courts, that preamble shows that the purpose of the law is not to thwart Kyoto—but to genuinely produce as much environmentally and socially clean energy as possible. This will benefit Albertans economically and environmentally and benefit the world environmentally. If the Clean Energy Act were to have as its avowed purpose the frustration of Kyoto, the courts could say that the law was just opportunistically using section 92A, and that the true purpose was not energy production.

Besides being legally important, the preamble also tells a story for the public—a story that has been stifled in the media debate over Kyoto. Alberta energy—and indeed all Canadian industries—are among the cleanest and most ethical in the world. Any federal law that puts Canadian industries at an economic disadvantage merely serve to drive that business to less respectable locales. The argument is as true for Hamilton's steel mills as it is for Fort McMurray's oil sands.

Section 4 of the Clean Energy Act outlines a mandatory minimum cumulative level of production for the province— so as to thwart any federal attempts to use Kyoto to reduce energy production. This section is not designed to artificially require companies to produce more than they naturally would. Section 3 allows any company to adjust their production levels as they choose. Essentially, the Clean Energy Act allows companies to turn their own production plans into provincial law, and change those plans as they see fit.

Finally, section 7 of the Clean Energy Act is a way for the Minister of Energy to sing the praises of the industry, and to point out success stories. For example, until it recently announced its sale, Calgary-based Talisman Energy was the only socially responsible oil company in a four-nation consortium in Sudan, a country beset by civil war. While Talisman's partners—including China—didn't care about human rights in Sudan, Talisman took it upon itself to spend millions of dollars on local development in that country, including setting up medical clinics, and even an entrepreneurship school for Sudanese women.[268]

---

[268] *2001 Annual Report*, Talisman Energy Inc., Calgary, 2002, p. 16.

That's the thing about Kyoto: None of Talisman's partners in the Sudan project have to make emissions reductions under Kyoto. So if Kyoto would have driven Talisman out of the Sudan—or out of business altogether—the environment wouldn't have been any cleaner, not one less drop of oil would have been sold, but an exporter of Canadian humanitarian values would have been snuffed out by Ottawa. The Clean Energy Act's annual report would be a public relations tool to remind Canadians—and the world—that we are already the cleanest, most ethical energy producers now. We didn't need Kyoto to tell us to be that way, and Kyoto won't help one whit.

We are already the cleanest, most ethical energy producers now. We didn't need Kyoto to tell us to be that way, and Kyoto won't help one whit.

Everything in the Clean Energy Act could be adopted, for example, for Ontario's electricity industry. Like Alberta, Ontario has an enviable record of safety, cleanliness and community ethics. There's no need to replace a made in Ontario culture of energy responsibility with a made in Japan treaty designed more to squeeze foreign aid out of Canada than to reduce pollution.

As *Fight Kyoto* goes to print, no province has a Clean Energy Act-style law in place. But on November 19, 2002 the Government of Alberta rolled out their proposed version of a shark cage law—called the Climate Change and Emissions Management Bill, or Bill 32.[269]

That proposed law does not specifically refer to section 92A of the Constitution, and it doesn't set minimum pro-

---

[269] Bill 32, *Climate Change and Emissions Management Act*, Legislative Assembly of Alberta, November, 2002.

duction levels for oil and gas. The bill contains detailed outlines for implementing the province's Kyoto Lite, including emissions trading, sinks and other Kyoto-style provisions. But the heart of the bill is section 3(3), which states that the "specified gas emission targets established under this Act are the only specified gas emission targets in effect in Alberta"—signalling to Ottawa that any Kyoto laws the Liberals might try to implement would violate Alberta laws enacted first.

Shoe-horning "emissions" into section 92A might be a stretch; and the bill does not specifically promote the most energy production possible. But Alberta's bill is a clear message to the federal government—and a clear example for other provinces—that foisting Kyoto on the country will take more than just whipping a hundred Liberal back-bench MPs into submission.

CHAPTER TWENTY-ONE

What Does the Future Hold?

If Paul Martin becomes the next Canadian Prime Minister—which seems inevitable—will he continue the implementation of the Kyoto Protocol? It is impossible to predict the future, but Martin's statements when he was the Liberal party's Environment Critic in the early 1990s shows that he has a disturbing penchant for mimicking the environmental one-worldism of his old boss and mentor, Maurice Strong.

> Maintaining low environmental standards for the purpose of attracting economic investment should be regarded as an unacceptable subsidy, subject to the same economic sanctions as any other unacceptable subsidy,

Martin wrote in a *Toronto Star* column in 1992.[270] He criticized the North American Free Trade Agreement because:

> It does not resolve a situation where one NAFTA member holds a competitive advantage over other members because it has not signed an international environmental convention.

In particular, Martin condemned the United States for not jumping on Strong's Rio Earth Summit bandwagon, and

---

[270] Paul Martin, "Trade deal fails to reconcile environment, economy," *The Toronto Star*, October 8, 1992, p. A25.

lamented the fact that "the Americans now have an advantage" in attracting investments. Instead of declining to commit Canada to UN treaties, Martin wanted to punish the U.S. for not signing them too.

Ten years later, in September 2002, Martin told *The Toronto Star* that his environmental zeal had not waned, and that he wanted to start implementing Kyoto as soon as possible. "I don't think that you should spend the next number of years working that plan out,"[271] he said.

> The fact is that there are targets. And if you're going to meet them, then you've got to begin work on them right away.

Martin gave the standard Liberal line about the pain of Kyoto being spread out—"regionally fair" as he calls it, the kind of Kyoto taxes, for example, that would hit all Canadians at the gas pump, rather than just targeting Alberta's oil companies. That's what passes for reasonable in Ottawa these days: promising to spread the recession to every Canadian, not just to Alberta. It's a political strategy that probably won't win Martin many points in the West, but it should scare any Ontarian or Quebecker who likes to drive or heat their home in the winter.

That's what passes for reasonable in Ottawa these days: promising to spread the recession to every Canadian, not just to Alberta.

"Yes, I would like to see Kyoto ratified," Martin told the *Star*.

---

271 Graham Fraser, "Liberals can't delay Kyoto plan, Martin says," *The Toronto Star*, September 26, 2002 p. A6.

Though just a back-bencher since being fired from cabinet, Martin has been on a bit of a Kyoto road show. He scheduled an interview with the CBC to say:

> I think it's very, very important that, in fact, that we deal with climate change, but that we set out the plan by which Canada can achieve its objectives.[272]

He told CTV's Ken Shaw "for those of us who believe in Kyoto, you want to know there's a plan to do it."[273] He doesn't just support Kyoto. He *believes* in it.

Paul Martin's reputation is that of a blue Liberal—a businessman himself, who does not indulge ideological wars against industry for the fun of it, as his more radical predecessors have, and his colleagues might. For nearly nine years he strengthened that reputation, by slowly managing the federal budget back into balance.

But if Martin becomes Prime Minister—an inevitability, if pundits are to be believed—he will no longer be able to confine himself to the role of fiscal watchdog. As Finance Minister, he could play the role of the cost-conscious hawk, for he was balanced out by the likes of Allan Rock and Sheila Copps, on the interventionist side of the party. As Prime Minister—and perhaps more so in the 2004 federal election campaign, and the Liberal leadership race, if there is one—he will likely try to prove that he is more than just a penny-pinching businessman.

"Most people don't realize just what a one-trick pony Martin was in cabinet," opines Lorne Gunter.

---

272 Paul Martin, *The National*, CBC, August 25, 2002.

273 Paul Martin, *CFTO TV*, September 25, 2002.

He was great at Finance, but seemed to have few ideas on any other subject. Martin has said no implementation without a plan first. That's good. But he is prone to impulsive concessions to his party's left-wing, just to prove he is socially aware and responsible.

As a cabinet minister in the government that signed Kyoto, and that campaigned on global warming in two election campaigns' Red Books, it might prove difficult for Martin to abandon a program that he is already politically wedded to. Says Gunter:

> I wouldn't put it past him to try, sincerely, to implement Kyoto if it were already ratified by the time he gets into office…That's another reason Kyoto has to be stopped now.

Paul Martin's already got the business vote, and he has no shortage of campaign contributors. What he needs now is to show his liberal side—the idealistic, big-dreaming, big government side. And Kyoto—or at least the distorted public perception of Kyoto—meets that need handily.

Do the math: 119 Liberal MPs issued a press release, demanding that Kyoto be ratified immediately. Public opinion polls still show Kyoto is popular—and even in Alberta, the public wants some form of action.

The media, especially the CBC, are cheerleading for Kyoto, and any politician who supports it. And, with the Bloc Quebecois and the New Democrats in favour of Kyoto—and the Tories taking a middle-of-the road approach—he has political cover for proceeding. At the federal political level, only the Canadian Alliance is heartily opposed.

Martin backed the Rio Earth Summit. For half a century, he has been a close friend of Rio's chairman, and the wizard behind Kyoto: Maurice Strong. He has repeatedly said he want implementation—and fast.

Will he do it?

Will he pull the trigger?

As the National Energy Program taught us, sometimes it's best to take the Liberal party at its word, especially when it's members are talking about massive new taxes and spending programs, things they like to do in any event.

As the National Energy Program taught us, sometimes it's better to take the Liberal party at its word.

Besides, Jean Chrétien, the departing Prime Minister, just might pull the trigger for him.

None of Martin's reasons for saying "no" apply to Chrétien. Unlike Martin, Chrétien doesn't have to appease the West, or industry anymore. He doesn't have to watch opinion polls, because he's not running for office. Instead, he can focus on building a "legacy," like Pierre Trudeau did.

If Chrétien were to leave office without Kyoto in place, what would he be remembered for, in the history books? Balancing the budget? That's hardly a stirring political epitaph—and it's one that Martin himself would probably claim for his own. Nearly losing the 1995 Quebec referendum? A string of ethical lapses in his cabinet? Getting a government loan for a Shawinigan golf course?

No, that's not the stuff of history. But ratifying and implementing the Kyoto Protocol, well that isn't just historical, it's global. And while it may elicit squawking in some business quarters in Canada, it would turn him into a global hero. Indeed, when Chrétien announced his intentions to ratify Kyoto, he did not do so in Parliament, or even at a key Canadian speech. He made the announcement at the United Nations convention in Johannesburg—all the better to bask in the global glory, and to win favour of the Kyotocrats at the UN.

For while Chrétien is nearly done as Canada's Prime Minister, he still brims with energy and ambition. He would run again as Liberal leader if he could, but he can't; he would undo Martin, his successor, if he could, and he has done his best so far. Ratifying Kyoto and enacting legislation to implement it—and leaving Martin to either follow through and bear the economic burden, or tear up the deal and lose face—is perhaps the perfect finale to Chrétien's parliamentary career, and the perfect entry into a UN career.

Jean Chrétien, UN Secretary-General? Scolding Paul Martin, the Prime Minister of Canada for not going far enough on Kyoto? That could be the future for Canada.

Kyoto could be the future if provincial governments lose their courage to fight.

Kyoto could be the future, even if the provinces fight, but if they don't fight smart—if they challenge Kyoto in the courts, on the federal government's terms, instead of on section 92A grounds.

If Canadians arm themselves with the facts about Kyoto, there is a chance to fight and win.

Kyoto could be the future if the grinding, daily propaganda from the Kyoto fundamentalists continues, from the CBC and government-funded environmentalist groups, such as the Federation of Canadian Municipalities. But if Canadians arm themselves with the facts about Kyoto, there is a chance to fight and win. To tell people that Kyoto isn't just about Alberta, but that every province will be hurt, from offshore rig workers in Newfoundland to auto makers in Windsor, to dairy farmers in Quebec. To tell well-intentioned Canadians who care about clean air that Kyoto doesn't deal with pollution at all—it only limits harmless carbon dioxide and methane, leaving smog and other chemicals out. To tell taxpayers that they'll be hit at the gas pump, in their monthly heating bills and their daily parking fees—all to pay for imaginary "credits" from foreign countries.

That's our chance.

It's not too late.

Now let's go fight Kyoto.

Fight Kyoto—
The Debater's Guide

Whether you find yourself fighting Kyoto over the water-cooler at your office, at a Rotary Club luncheon, or in the House of Commons, odds are you will hear the same, shop-worn arguments. In fact, you'd be lucky to hear *arguments* at all—the fervour of many pro-Kyoto Canadians borders on blind faith. That means the hardest part of any Kyoto debate will likely be steering your opponent away from personal insults and towards the science, economics or other facts.

Here are the top ten Kyoto fibs, rebutted with a fact-check. Following that is a list of four secrets Canadians should know about Kyoto.

TOP TEN KYOTO FIBS

1. *Fib:* The Kyoto Protocol is our last chance to save the planet.

   Fact: Even pro-Kyoto scientists concede that if every country in the world obeyed Kyoto, the total difference in global warming would only be 0.2 degrees Celsius by the year 2100.

2. *Fib:* Over 150 countries have signed Kyoto—we have to do our part.

   Fact: Most countries that have signed the Kyoto Protocol don't have to reduce their emissions at all. Canada would be the only country in North or South

America that has to made any reductions—while industrial countries like the U.S., China, India, Brazil, Mexico and the OPEC countries don't.

3. *Fib:*   If we don't sign the Kyoto Protocol, Canada will be embarrassed internationally.

   Fact: Canada has nothing to be embarrassed about—dollar for dollar, our economy is already one of the world's cleanest, and we're getting cleaner every year. If Canada were to implement Kyoto, the government's taxes and regulations would actually drive industries to countries that are dirtier than Canada.

4. *Fib:*   Scientists all agree: global warming is a threat to the planet.

   Fact: Even the official United Nations scientific panel, called the IPCC, admits that human-caused global warming is just a theory, not a proven fact. And the largest global warming study ever taken—23 years of satellite readings—shows that the total warming over that time period is just 0.06 degrees Celsius per decade. The Earth's climate naturally changes—and has for millions of years.

       Ordinary Canadians are skeptical, too: a November 2002 Environics poll shows that only 20 per cent of Canadians believe the Kyoto science is settled.

5. *Fib:*   Global warming is already causing more hurricanes, tornadoes and droughts.

   Fact: According to the UN's IPCC science panel, there is no proof that storms are getting bigger or more frequent. What has changed is that more real estate development on coastlines means that when a hurricane does hit, it causes more property damage than it would have a century ago. And the proliferation of video cameras and the advent of 24-hour news channels means that no storm event goes unnoticed.

6. *Fib:* The only people opposed to Kyoto are oil company executives.

   Fact: Kyoto will hurt Canada's energy industry. But it will also hurt the auto industry, steel industry, transportation industry and, surprisingly, agriculture—livestock, like humans, emit large amounts of gas. Any business that needs energy will be hurt—and Canadians who use energy to fuel their cars or heat their homes will pay, too.

7. *Fib:* Canada is one of the world's biggest users of energy—more than our share.

   Fact: Canada is a cold country, so it is natural that we would need more energy to heat our homes in the winter than they would in balmy Portugal; we are a large country, so we would need more energy to travel within our country than they would in tiny Luxembourg.

8. *Fib:* Kyoto won't cost us any jobs—it will create jobs in high tech new industries.

   Fact: Kyoto has already cost Canadian jobs—for example, major oil sands plants have announced that they are suspending new construction because of Kyoto. The government is counting on miracle technologies, that do not exist and are not even on the drawing board, to make Kyoto pay. So far, though, cold fusion and other solutions are just the stuff of science fiction.

9. *Fib:* We have been debating Kyoto for five years—let's just get on with it, already.

Fact: Canada signed the Kyoto treaty back in 1997 without a vote in Parliament. Government hearings on the subject have deliberately excluded Kyoto opponents. Every provincial government in the country has opposed the federal government's unilateral approach. And a majority of Canadians want more information before proceeding.

10. *Fib:*   Canada's environment is getting dirtier every year—we have to do something.

Fact: Canada's environment has been getting cleaner every year for a generation—if the measurement is in terms of true pollution. Sulphur dioxide, water pollution, lead pollution—all have been reduced. Kyoto will only cut down on carbon dioxide, a harmless gas. But it will drive businesses to less clean countries that don't have Kyoto rules.

FOUR MORE SECRETS ABOUT KYOTO

1. Kyoto is a treaty about foreign aid.

The Kyoto Protocol says that if countries can't reduce their emissions on their own, they must pay other countries cash. Canada's own Kyoto draft plan involves sending billions of dollars a year to countries like Russia and the Ukraine, who have extra emissions "credits" to sell.

2. Kyoto limits Canada's sovereignty to make our own national choices.

Kyoto requires Canada's economy to stay still: It does not allow us to grow our energy use to accept new immigrants or new businesses. If we want to use more energy than pre-1990 levels, we need to buy permission from other countries, with cash.

3. Kyoto could break up the country.

Opinion polls show that half of Albertans would consider

separating from Canada if the Kyoto treaty was implemented. It's not an idle threat—Alberta spawned a separatist party during the National Energy Program, and even elected a separatist to the provincial legislature.

4. If we want to help the environment, there are smarter ways to do it.

If every developed nation in the world spent just one year's worth of Kyoto costs on solving real pollution problems instead, everyone in the Third World could have clean drinking water and sanitation.

The Annotated Kyoto Protocol

On December 10, 1997 the Kyoto Protocol was born. Here is the text of the Kyoto Protocol, as well as an analysis of its most controversial and troublesome clauses:

Kyoto Protocol to the United Nations Framework Convention on Climate Change
December 10, 1997

The Parties to this Protocol, Being Parties to the United Nations Framework Convention on Climate Change, hereinafter referred to as "the Convention," In pursuit of the ultimate objective of the Convention as stated in its Article 2, Recalling the provisions of the Convention, Being guided by Article 3 of the Convention, Pursuant to the Berlin Mandate adopted by decision 1/CP.1 of the Conference of the Parties to the Convention at its first session, Have agreed as follows:

Analysis: The "Framework Convention on Climate Change" was adopted at UN headquarters in New York on May 9, 1992. The next month, foreign diplomats and politicians—including Brian Mulroney, Paul Martin and Ralph Klein—converged on Rio de Janeiro, where Canada and other countries signed the treaty. Within a year, 166 nations had done so.

This Convention—commonly called "Rio"—was an internally inconsistent treaty.

For example, the "ultimate objective" of Article 2 of Rio was

"stabilization of greenhouse gas concentrations in the atmosphere"—but also "to enable economic development to proceed in a sustainable manner."

Article 3 of Rio was even more confusing. It said "developed" countries should bear most of the burden of cutting back on emissions. But it also said any country that "would have to bear a disproportionate or abnormal burden...should be given full consideration."

Rio said that "economic development is essential" and that any environmental policy "should be cost-effective so as to ensure global benefits at the lowest possible cost."

But it also said that "lack of full scientific certainty should not be used as a reason for postponing such measures."

In the spring of 1995, the eco-diplomats flew to Berlin. By this point, the contradictions in Rio were obvious—as was the fact that each country was waiting for the other to start cutting back on emissions. In Berlin, the diplomats agreed that the Rio treaty was "not adequate" and that it was time to "take appropriate action for the period beyond 2000, including the strengthening of the commitments" for developed countries. This led the way for Kyoto, in 1997.

Article 1
For the purposes of this Protocol, the definitions contained in Article 1 of the Convention shall apply. In addition:
1. "Conference of the Parties" means the Conference of the Parties to the Convention.
2. "Convention" means the United Nations Framework Convention on Climate Change, adopted in New York on 9 May 1992.
3. "Intergovernmental Panel on Climate Change" means the Intergovernmental Panel on Climate Change established in 1988 jointly by the World Meteorological Organization and the United Nations Environment Programme.

Analysis: The very name "Intergovernmental Panel on Climate Change" contains a rhetorical conclusion: that the climate is indeed changing. Nonetheless, this politically-appointed body of scientists has been held up as an impartial authority vouching for the theory of global warming. The fact is, the science is inconclusive.

4. "Montreal Protocol" means the Montreal Protocol on Substances that Deplete the Ozone Layer, adopted in Montreal on 16 September 1987 and as subsequently adjusted and amended.

5. "Parties present and voting" means Parties present and casting an affirmative or negative vote.

6. "Party" means, unless the context otherwise indicates, a Party to this Protocol.

Analysis: "Party" is the UN word for "country." But taxpayers could be forgiven for thinking it referred to the constant junkets that eco-diplomats are on. Over the last ten years, eco-diplomats have been to grandly-named conferences in New York, Rio, Berlin, Geneva, Kyoto, Buenos Aires, Bratislava (Slovakia), Marrakech (Morocco), Nairobi, The Hague, Bali (Indonesia), Johannesburg, and New Delhi—just to name the big ones.

7. "Party included in Annex I" means a Party included in Annex I to the Convention, as may be amended, or a Party which has made a notification under Article 4, paragraph 2(g), of the Convention.

Analysis: Article 4, paragraph 2(g) of Rio is how countries sign up for emission reductions. Article 4—which was written in 1992—calls for emission reductions "by the end of the present decade." Of course, we are well into the next decade, but that's not bad news for UN's jet-setting diplomatic class—it just means more trips to more exotic locales, for endless annual reunions with the same junketeers. Think of it as a high school reunion—but held every year, in another exciting country, at another 5-star hotel...and paid for by taxpayers.

Question: How much greenhouse gas is released just flying all of these very important diplomats and politicians from a hundred countries to these interminable conferences every six or eight months?

Article 2
1. Each Party included in Annex I, in achieving its quantified emission limitation and reduction commitments under Article 3, in order to promote sustainable development, shall:

Analysis: Annex 1 is the bureaucratic name for the list that contains developed countries and developing countries that are not expected to bear the economic burden of reducing greenhouse gases. Like the membership of the IPCC, the list of developed countries is a political statement in itself. Russia is on this list of poor countries, even though it is a permanent member of the UN Security Council, a member of the G-8 and a nuclear power. Turkey, on the other hand, found itself in the Annex II list, which only contains developed countries, making Turkey responsible for the economic costs of emission reductions alongside clearly wealthier countries such as Switzerland and Germany.

(a) Implement and/or further elaborate policies and measures in accordance with its national circumstances, such as:
(i) Enhancement of energy efficiency in relevant sectors of the national economy;

Analysis: Although Canada uses more energy per person than many other countries, we use that energy far more efficiently—and become more efficient every year.

(ii) Protection and enhancement of sinks and reservoirs of greenhouse gases not controlled by the Montreal Protocol, taking into account its commitments under relevant international environmental agreements; promotion of sustainable forest management practices, afforestation and reforestation;

Analysis: "Sinks" and "reservoirs" are a fudge-factor in Kyoto. Trees and pretty much anything else that's green consume carbon dioxide—the most abundant greenhouse gas—and emit oxygen. Calling Canada's forests a carbon sink is essentially an accounting trick: can we get credit for reducing our emissions, just by pointing to those trees? If so, Canada, and other florid countries won't have to do as much to comply with Rio or Kyoto. But if this endless series of UN meetings was actually just a political debate among accountants and lobbyists—and not really about the environment—then the charade should end. Energy consumers should feel relieved; environmental activists should feel betrayed; and taxpayers should demand their money back for the UN's traveling gourmands.

The irony of the Annex I and Annex II country classification, is that the Annex II developed countries are, dollar for dollar and pound for pound, far cleaner and more energy efficient than the developing countries. The only feasible way for Canada to meet our Kyoto emission reductions would be to stop doing things—to stop driving from Montreal to Toronto or from Calgary to Edmonton; to stop heating our homes above 15 degrees Celsius in the winter; to stop the assembly lines at the GM plant. All of these Canadian activities are already world leaders in efficiency and are improving as fast as science and economics will allow

The Annex I countries, on the other hand, have tremendous room for environmental improvement—not because of their level of industrial activity, but because of the inefficiencies in their obsolete economies.

Kyoto puts the burden solely on the Annex II countries to make improvements—and ignores the low-hanging fruit in developed countries. Scrubbing that last one per cent of pollution out of a modern, efficient Canadian factory would cost more and accomplish less than scrubbing 90 per cent of the pollution out of a Mao-era factory in China.

(iii) Promotion of sustainable forms of agriculture in light of climate change considerations;
(iv) Research on, and promotion, development and increased use of, new and renewable forms of energy, of carbon dioxide sequestration technologies and of advanced and innovative environmentally sound technologies;

Analysis: Placing all one's bets on research and development is the secular equivalent of just plain old praying for help. Researchers have been working on cold fusion and other alchemy for decades, but it seems their only success has been at clinching government grants—the fruits of R & D are usually incremental, and slow, and are rarely the result of a political edict. Even the largest research projects in the world—such as the American moon landing—take years to bear results. Kyoto's deadlines will come and go before that cycle is complete.

Of course R & D into cleaner and more efficient technology should continue—and it is, at the expense and direction of Canadian companies that reinvest their profits. It is that corporate R & D, for example, that has cut the cost and the environmental emissions from Alberta's massive oil sands project. But the first item in a corporate budget that will be cut in a Kyoto recession will be such long-term, risky investments. An oil company or steel plant that is grappling with bankruptcy today will not likely spend money on basic research for tomorrow.

(v) Progressive reduction or phasing out of market imperfections, fiscal incentives, tax and duty exemptions and subsidies in all greenhouse gas emitting sectors that run counter to the objective of the Convention and application of market instruments;
(vi) Encouragement of appropriate reforms in relevant sectors aimed at promoting policies and measures which limit or reduce emissions of greenhouse gases not controlled by the Montreal Protocol;

Analysis: This is the guts of Kyoto: reducing emissions of greenhouse gases. It sounds innocuous—"encouragement" is the word that's used—but that encouragement will take the form of coercion, if it is to be effective. Families, businesses and factories will have to use less energy than they would otherwise choose to use voluntarily. The only way to make people do what they don't want to do is through taxes, regulations, rationing and other laws.

Get ready for the new Prohibition—but instead of alcohol that's banned, oil is.

Carbon dioxide is the main "greenhouse gas" that Kyoto addresses—which makes anyone who exhales an "emission source." People are a source of methane emissions, too—but that is not a fact mentioned in polite company.

> (vii) Measures to limit and/or reduce emissions of greenhouse gases not controlled by the Montreal Protocol in the transport sector;
> (viii) Limitation and/or reduction of methane emissions through recovery and use in waste management, as well as in the production, transport and distribution of energy;
> (b) Cooperate with other such Parties to enhance the individual and combined effectiveness of their policies and measures adopted under this Article, pursuant to Article 4, paragraph 2(e)(i), of the Convention. To this end, these Parties shall take steps to share their experience and exchange information on such policies and measures, including developing ways of improving their comparability, transparency and effectiveness. The Conference of the Parties serving as the meeting of the Parties to this Protocol shall, at its first session or as soon as practicable thereafter, consider ways to facilitate such cooperation, taking into account all relevant information.
> 2. The Parties included in Annex I shall pursue limitation or reduction of emissions of greenhouse gases not controlled by the Montreal Protocol from aviation and marine bunker fuels, working through the International

Civil Aviation Organization and the International Maritime Organization, respectively.

3. The Parties included in Annex I shall strive to implement policies and measures under this Article in such a way as to minimize adverse effects, including the adverse effects of climate change, effects on international trade, and social, environmental and economic impacts on other Parties, especially developing country Parties and in particular those identified in Article 4, paragraphs 8 and 9, of the Convention, taking into account Article 3 of the Convention. The Conference of the Parties serving as the meeting of the Parties to this Protocol may take further action, as appropriate, to promote the implementation of the provisions of this paragraph.

Analysis: This section allows Annex I countries—both rich and poor—to minimize social and economic impacts of Kyoto. By definition, reducing energy use by 30 per cent will have a massive economic and social impact—even if Kyoto's hopeful reliance on the magic of undiscovered miracle technologies comes true.

4. The Conference of the Parties serving as the meeting of the Parties to this Protocol, if it decides that it would be beneficial to coordinate any of the policies and measures in paragraph 1(a) above, taking into account different national circumstances and potential effects, shall consider ways and means to elaborate the coordination of such policies and measures.

Article 3

1. The Parties included in Annex I shall, individually or jointly, ensure that their aggregate anthropogenic carbon dioxide equivalent emissions of the greenhouse gases listed in Annex A do not exceed their assigned amounts, calculated pursuant to their quantified emission limitation and reduction commitments inscribed in Annex B and in accordance with the provisions of this Article,

with a view to reducing their overall emissions of such gases by at least 5 per cent below 1990 levels in the commitment period 2008 to 2012.

Analysis: Anthropogenic means human-created—but even cow flatulence is considered anthropogenic, since humans are the farmers.

Kyoto, however, is anthropocentric—too focused on humans. It totally ignores natural fluctuations in carbon dioxide and other emissions, from sources ranging from natural forest fires, to volcanoes.

Annex I and II are lists of countries. Annex A is a list of different gases determined to be greenhouse gases, and industrial sources of those gases. Annex B is a list of countries, with their emissions targets, using 1990 as a base year.

Conspicuously absent from Annex A's list of pollution, however, is the number one factor in air quality around the world—especially in developing countries. It's called "particulate pollution"—particles in the air, often seen in big cities in developing countries. The reason for particulate pollution varies from city to city; often, it is the result of thousands of small, inefficient family furnaces and braziers burning dirty fuel. It is particulate pollution—and not carbon dioxide—that darkens the sky and causes bronchitis and other lung disease. Don't tell that to the drafters of Kyoto, though—they're cracking down on their specific list of greenhouse gases, though medical science has not yet found a case of lung cancer caused by too much carbon dioxide.

Even if Kyoto did target particulate pollution, however, the great, polluted cities of the developing world—from Calcutta to Mexico City—would be exempt, because they are countries listed in Annex 1.

Annex B lists each country and the level of greenhouse gases it must achieve by the end of the decade, expressed as a per cent of their emissions in 1990. Canada, for example, must be at 94 per cent of 1990 levels, a six per cent reduction. Australia, by comparison, is allowed to emit eight per cent more than it did in 1990.

That's no favour for Australia, though—it's on track to exceed its 1990 levels by at least 11%, making even that seemingly lax target all but impossible to achieve. Better schedule another UN conference—anyone for Maui?

Kyoto gives countries a flexible deadline for reaching their respective reductions—anytime between 2008 to 2012. But Kyoto also says that "demonstrable progress" must be made by 2005— just two years away.

> 2. Each Party included in Annex I shall, by 2005, have made demonstrable progress in achieving its commitments under this Protocol.
> 3. The net changes in greenhouse gas emissions by sources and removals by sinks resulting from direct human-induced land-use change and forestry activities, limited to afforestation, reforestation and deforestation since 1990, measured as verifiable changes in carbon stocks in each commitment period, shall be used to meet the commitments under this Article of each Party included in Annex I. The greenhouse gas emissions by sources and removals by sinks associated with those activities shall be reported in a transparent and verifiable manner and reviewed in accordance with Articles 7 and 8.

Analysis: This section requires that countries' emissions reductions be measured, reported and verified. Makes sense— there is no point trying to quantify targets, as Kyoto does, without having a measuring system.

But who will be in charge of measuring each country's emissions? What standards will they use? What will count, and what won't? And even if those issues can be addressed in the next few years, how are 1990 level emissions—the base year for calculating reductions—to be calculated, when reliable data is not available for most countries back then? (In some cases, countries that existed in 1990 no longer do; and other countries have been born since then.)

These vicissitudes, that will be decided over cocktails at the next UN retreat, will mean the difference between success and failure for thousands of companies in Canada.

4. Prior to the first session of the Conference of the Parties serving as the meeting of the Parties to this Protocol, each Party included in Annex I shall provide, for consideration by the Subsidiary Body for Scientific and Technological Advice, data to establish its level of carbon stocks in 1990 and to enable an estimate to be made of its changes in carbon stocks in subsequent years. The Conference of the Parties serving as the meeting of the Parties to this Protocol shall, at its first session or as soon as practicable thereafter, decide upon modalities, rules and guidelines as to how, and which, additional human-induced activities related to changes in green-house gas emissions by sources and removals by sinks in the agricultural soils and the land-use change and forestry categories shall be added to, or subtracted from, the assigned amounts for Parties included in Annex I, taking into account uncertainties, transparency in reporting, ver-ifiability, the methodological work of the Intergovernmental Panel on Climate Change, the advice provided by the Subsidiary Body for Scientific and Technological Advice in accordance with Article 5 and the decisions of the Conference of the Parties. Such a decision shall apply in the second and subsequent com-mitment periods. A Party may choose to apply such a decision on these additional human-induced activities for its first commitment period, provided that these activities have taken place since 1990.

Analysis: This provision allows Kyoto countries to guesstimate their emission levels in 1990. The natural incentive for each country is to overstate and exaggerate, wherever pos-sible, the levels of carbon emitted in 1990, so that reducing emis-sions from that artificially high level is easier and less costly to do.

For some countries—such as the former East Germany—emissions in 1990 were genuinely awful, as that country emerged from fifty years of Soviet-style industrial pollution. Just the natural phasing out and cleaning up of Soviet-era, smoke-belching plants would allow the united Germany to achieve its reduction goals. That, of course, is the reason for Germany's exuberant support for Kyoto—the treaty will impose economic restrictions on other countries that it will be immune from itself.

Other European countries will benefit from absorbing East Germany, too, because the European Union "declared" that its member countries would be judged together on emissions levels "in the Community as a whole." Because of this, Kyoto won't have a significant impact on Europe; but it will have a significant impact on Europe's economic competitors—such as Canada and the U.S.—if those countries enact it. That is precisely the economic danger that the U.S. Senate unanimously opposed in a July 1997 vote—but a danger to which Canada still seems oblivious.

5. The Parties included in Annex I undergoing the process of transition to a market economy whose base year or period was established pursuant to decision 9/CP.2 of the Conference of the Parties at its second session shall use that base year or period for the implementation of their commitments under this Article. Any other Party included in Annex I undergoing the process of transition to a market economy which has not yet submitted its first national communication under Article 12 of the Convention may also notify the Conference of the Parties serving as the meeting of the Parties to this Protocol that it intends to use an historical base year or period other than 1990 for the implementation of its commitments under this Article. The Conference of the Parties serving as the meeting of the Parties to this Protocol shall decide on the acceptance of such notification.

Analysis: This section specifically spells out that former Soviet-bloc countries can choose their liberation dates as their starting point for emission reductions. In a sense this is fair—until the liberation, these countries were totalitarian regimes that did not value environmental or economic freedom. The effect of this, however, is to give these countries the dirtiest possible standard upon which to improve—and therefore the maximum possible economic advantage over Canada and other Annex II developed countries.

6. Taking into account Article 4, paragraph 6, of the Convention, in the implementation of their commitments under this Protocol other than those under this Article, a certain degree of flexibility shall be allowed by the Conference of the Parties serving as the meeting of the Parties to this Protocol to the Parties included in Annex I undergoing the process of transition to a market economy.

Analysis: This paragraph refers to the "certain degree of flexibility" that the Rio treaty gave to former Soviet-bloc countries.

7. In the first quantified emission limitation and reduction commitment period, from 2008 to 2012, the assigned amount for each Party included in Annex I shall be equal to the percentage inscribed for it in Annex B of its aggregate anthropogenic carbon dioxide equivalent emissions of the greenhouse gases listed in Annex A in 1990, or the base year or period determined in accordance with paragraph 5 above, multiplied by five. Those Parties included in Annex I for whom land-use change and forestry constituted a net source of greenhouse gas emissions in 1990 shall include in their 1990 emissions base year or period the aggregate anthropogenic carbon dioxide equivalent emissions by sources minus removals by sinks in 1990 from land-use change for the purposes of calculating their assigned amount.

8. Any Party included in Annex I may use 1995 as its base year for hydrofluorocarbons, perfluorocarbons and

sulphur hexafluoride, for the purposes of the calculation referred to in paragraph 7 above.

9. Commitments for subsequent periods for Parties included in Annex I shall be established in amendments to Annex B to this Protocol, which shall be adopted in accordance with the provisions of Article 21, paragraph 7. The Conference of the Parties serving as the meeting of the Parties to this Protocol shall initiate the consideration of such commitments at least seven years before the end of the first commitment period referred to in paragraph 1 above.

10. Any emission reduction units, or any part of an assigned amount, which a Party acquires from another Party in accordance with the provisions of Article 6 or of Article 17 shall be added to the assigned amount for the acquiring Party.

Analysis: These are the sections that allow "emissions trading"—where high emissions countries may acquire pollution credits from low-emissions countries. This acquisition, of course, would not be free—the right to emit carbon dioxide would have to be bought from those who had extra rights left over.

The right to emit carbon dioxide—heretofore a right of anyone—is now a right that is rationed, and bought and sold. It has been artificially given a value by the UN, and so-called developing countries have artificially been given emissions quotas to hoard—while developed countries face an insuperable shortfall.

The effect of this is plain: Canada and other developed countries will have to send money to Russia and others countries for permission to keep using energy as we always have. Russia will not actually sell us anything material, nor any rights that Canadians do not currently enjoy. It is a completely fictitious trade, with nothing being received in consideration for the sale, other than the UN's approval. It is a roundabout way of increasing foreign aid, in the guise of environmentalism. Ironically, the countries that will pay for these credits are far more environmentally efficient than the countries being rewarded with the payment.

11. Any emission reduction units, or any part of an assigned amount, which a Party transfers to another Party in accordance with the provisions of Article 6 or of Article 17 shall be subtracted from the assigned amount for the transferring Party.

12. Any certified emission reductions which a Party acquires from another Party in accordance with the provisions of Article 12 shall be added to the assigned amount for the acquiring Party.

13. If the emissions of a Party included in Annex I in a commitment period are less than its assigned amount under this Article, this difference shall, on request of that Party, be added to the assigned amount for that Party for subsequent commitment periods.

Analysis: This provision allows a country that exceeds its emission reduction levels in one year, to get credit for that extra reduction in subsequent years.

14. Each Party included in Annex I shall strive to implement the commitments mentioned in paragraph 1 above in such a way as to minimize adverse social, environmental and economic impacts on developing country Parties, particularly those identified in Article 4, paragraphs 8 and 9, of the Convention. In line with relevant decisions of the Conference of the Parties on the implementation of those paragraphs, the Conference of the Parties serving as the meeting of the Parties to this Protocol shall, at its first session, consider what actions are necessary to minimize the adverse effects of climate change and/or the impacts of response measures on Parties referred to in those paragraphs. Among the issues to be considered shall be the establishment of funding, insurance and transfer of technology.

Article 4

1. Any Parties included in Annex I that have reached an agreement to fulfill their commitments under Article 3

jointly, shall be deemed to have met those commitments provided that their total combined aggregate anthropogenic carbon dioxide equivalent emissions of the greenhouse gases listed in Annex A do not exceed their assigned amounts calculated pursuant to their quantified emission limitation and reduction commitments inscribed in Annex B and in accordance with the provisions of Article 3. The respective emission level allocated to each of the Parties to the agreement shall be set out in that agreement.

Analysis: This provision specifically allows European countries to sop up any extra credit that the former East Germany would receive for shutting down Soviet-era factories.

2. The Parties to any such agreement shall notify the secretariat of the terms of the agreement on the date of deposit of their instruments of ratification, acceptance or approval of this Protocol, or accession thereto. The secretariat shall in turn inform the Parties and signatories to the Convention of the terms of the agreement.

3. Any such agreement shall remain in operation for the duration of the commitment period specified in Article 3, paragraph 7.

4. If Parties acting jointly do so in the framework of, and together with, a regional economic integration organization, any alteration in the composition of the organization after adoption of this Protocol shall not affect existing commitments under this Protocol. Any alteration in the composition of the organization shall only apply for the purposes of those commitments under Article 3 that are adopted subsequent to that alteration.

5. In the event of failure by the Parties to such an agreement to achieve their total combined level of emission reductions, each Party to that agreement shall be responsible for its own level of emissions set out in the agreement.

6. If Parties acting jointly do so in the framework of, and together with, a regional economic integration organization which is itself a Party to this Protocol, each member State of that regional economic integration organization individually, and together with the regional economic integration organization acting in accordance with Article 24, shall, in the event of failure to achieve the total combined level of emission reductions, be responsible for its level of emissions as notified in accordance with this Article.

Article 5

Analysis: These sections are an attempt to standardize the methods of measuring carbon dioxide.

1. Each Party included in Annex I shall have in place, no later than one year prior to the start of the first commitment period, a national system for the estimation of anthropogenic emissions by sources and removals by sinks of all greenhouse gases not controlled by the Montreal Protocol. Guidelines for such national systems, which shall incorporate the methodologies specified in paragraph 2 below, shall be decided upon by the Conference of the Parties serving as the meeting of the Parties to this Protocol at its first session.

2. Methodologies for estimating anthropogenic emissions by sources and removals by sinks of all greenhouse gases not controlled by the Montreal Protocol shall be those accepted by the Intergovernmental Panel on Climate Change and agreed upon by the Conference of the Parties at its third session. Where such methodologies are not used, appropriate adjustments shall be applied according to methodologies agreed upon by the Conference of the Parties serving as the meeting of the Parties to this Protocol at its first session. Based on the work of, inter alia, the Intergovernmental Panel on Climate Change and advice provided by the Subsidiary Body for Scientific and

Technological Advice, the Conference of the Parties serving as the meeting of the Parties to this Protocol shall regularly review and, as appropriate, revise such methodologies and adjustments, taking fully into account any relevant decisions by the Conference of the Parties. Any revision to methodologies or adjustments shall be used only for the purposes of ascertaining compliance with commitments under Article 3 in respect of any commitment period adopted subsequent to that revision.

3. The global warming potentials used to calculate the carbon dioxide equivalence of anthropogenic emissions by sources and removals by sinks of greenhouse gases listed in Annex A shall be those accepted by the Intergovernmental Panel on Climate Change and agreed upon by the Conference of the Parties at its third session. Based on the work of, inter alia, the Intergovernmental Panel on Climate Change and advice provided by the Subsidiary Body for Scientific and Technological Advice, the Conference of the Parties serving as the meeting of the Parties to this Protocol shall regularly review and, as appropriate, revise the global warming potential of each such greenhouse gas, taking fully into account any relevant decisions by the Conference of the Parties. Any revision to a global warming potential shall apply only to commitments under Article 3 in respect of any commitment period adopted subsequent to that revision.

Article 6

Analysis: This is the emissions trading section of Kyoto— another fudge-factor for countries that can't reduce emissions enough to meet their Kyoto targets. Stripping away the bureaucratic language, Article 6 simply allows countries to buy or bribe their way out of Kyoto emissions targets. Technically, countries such as Canada would actually be buying an emissions "credit"— but that credit is merely a legal fiction, an artificially created "right" to emit carbon dioxide, a right that Canada and all other countries already have.

It's foreign aid; nothing more, nothing less—and it's paid directly to developing countries, such as Russia.

1. For the purpose of meeting its commitments under Article 3, any Party included in Annex I may transfer to, or acquire from, any other such Party emission reduction units resulting from projects aimed at reducing anthropogenic emissions by sources or enhancing anthropogenic removals by sinks of greenhouse gases in any sector of the economy, provided that:

(a) Any such project has the approval of the Parties involved;

(b) Any such project provides a reduction in emissions by sources, or an enhancement of removals by sinks, that is additional to any that would otherwise occur;

(c) It does not acquire any emission reduction units if it is not in compliance with its obligations under Articles 5 and 7; and

(d) The acquisition of emission reduction units shall be supplemental to domestic actions for the purposes of meeting commitments under Article 3.

2. The Conference of the Parties serving as the meeting of the Parties to this Protocol may, at its first session or as soon as practicable thereafter, further elaborate guidelines for the implementation of this Article, including for verification and reporting.

3. A Party included in Annex I may authorize legal entities to participate, under its responsibility, in actions leading to the generation, transfer or acquisition under this Article of emission reduction units.

4. If a question of implementation by a Party included in Annex I of the requirements referred to in this Article is identified in accordance with the relevant provisions of Article 8, transfers and acquisitions of emission reduction units may continue to be made after the question has been identified, provided that any such units may not be used by a Party to meet its

commitments under Article 3 until any issue of compliance is resolved.

Article 7

1. Each Party included in Annex I shall incorporate in its annual inventory of anthropogenic emissions by sources and removals by sinks of greenhouse gases not controlled by the Montreal Protocol, submitted in accordance with the relevant decisions of the Conference of the Parties, the necessary supplementary information for the purposes of ensuring compliance with Article 3, to be determined in accordance with paragraph 4 below.

2. Each Party included in Annex I shall incorporate in its national communication, submitted under Article 12 of the Convention, the supplementary information necessary to demonstrate compliance with its commitments under this Protocol, to be determined in accordance with paragraph 4 below.

3. Each Party included in Annex I shall submit the information required under paragraph 1 above annually, beginning with the first inventory due under the Convention for the first year of the commitment period after this Protocol has entered into force for that Party. Each such Party shall submit the information required under paragraph 2 above as part of the first national communication due under the Convention after this Protocol has entered into force for it and after the adoption of guidelines as provided for in paragraph 4 below. The frequency of subsequent submission of information required under this Article shall be determined by the Conference of the Parties serving as the meeting of the Parties to this Protocol, taking into account any timetable for the submission of national communications decided upon by the Conference of the Parties.

4. The Conference of the Parties serving as the meeting of the Parties to this Protocol shall adopt at its first session, and review periodically thereafter, guidelines for the preparation of the information required under this

Article, taking into account guidelines for the preparation of national communications by Parties included in Annex I adopted by the Conference of the Parties. The Conference of the Parties serving as the meeting of the Parties to this Protocol shall also, prior to the first commitment period, decide upon modalities for the accounting of assigned amounts.

Article 8

1. The information submitted under Article 7 by each Party included in Annex I shall be reviewed by expert review teams pursuant to the relevant decisions of the Conference of the Parties and in accordance with guidelines adopted for this purpose by the Conference of the Parties serving as the meeting of the Parties to this Protocol under paragraph 4 below. The information submitted under Article 7, paragraph 1, by each Party included in Annex I shall be reviewed as part of the annual compilation and accounting of emissions inventories and assigned amounts. Additionally, the information submitted under Article 7, paragraph 2, by each Party included in Annex I shall be reviewed as part of the review of communications.

2. Expert review teams shall be coordinated by the secretariat and shall be composed of experts selected from those nominated by Parties to the Convention and, as appropriate, by intergovernmental organizations, in accordance with guidance provided for this purpose by the Conference of the Parties.

3. The review process shall provide a thorough and comprehensive technical assessment of all aspects of the implementation by a Party of this Protocol. The expert review teams shall prepare a report to the Conference of the Parties serving as the meeting of the Parties to this Protocol, assessing the implementation of the commitments of the Party and identifying any potential problems in, and factors influencing, the fulfillment of commitments. Such reports shall be circulated by the secretariat

to all Parties to the Convention. The secretariat shall list those questions of implementation indicated in such reports for further consideration by the Conference of the Parties serving as the meeting of the Parties to this Protocol.

4. The Conference of the Parties serving as the meeting of the Parties to this Protocol shall adopt at its first session, and review periodically thereafter, guidelines for the review of implementation of this Protocol by expert review teams taking into account the relevant decisions of the Conference of the Parties.

5. The Conference of the Parties serving as the meeting of the Parties to this Protocol shall, with the assistance of the Subsidiary Body for Implementation and, as appropriate, the Subsidiary Body for Scientific and Technological Advice, consider:

(a) The information submitted by Parties under Article 7 and the reports of the expert reviews thereon conducted under this Article; and

(b) Those questions of implementation listed by the secretariat under paragraph 3 above, as well as any questions raised by Parties.

6. Pursuant to its consideration of the information referred to in paragraph 5 above, the Conference of the Parties serving as the meeting of the Parties to this Protocol shall take decisions on any matter required for the implementation of this Protocol.

Article 9

1. The Conference of the Parties serving as the meeting of the Parties to this Protocol shall periodically review this Protocol in the light of the best available scientific information and assessments on climate change and its impacts, as well as relevant technical, social and economic information. Such reviews shall be coordinated with pertinent reviews under the Convention, in particular those required by Article 4, paragraph 2(d), and Article 7, paragraph 2(a), of the Convention. Based on

these reviews, the Conference of the Parties serving as the meeting of the Parties to this Protocol shall take appropriate action.

2. The first review shall take place at the second session of the Conference of the Parties serving as the meeting of the Parties to this Protocol. Further reviews shall take place at regular intervals and in a timely manner.

Article 10

All Parties, taking into account their common but differentiated responsibilities and their specific national and regional development priorities, objectives and circumstances, without introducing any new commitments for Parties not included in Annex I, but reaffirming existing commitments under Article 4, paragraph 1, of the Convention, and continuing to advance the implementation of these commitments in order to achieve sustainable development, taking into account Article 4, paragraphs 3, 5 and 7, of the Convention, shall:

(a) Formulate, where relevant and to the extent possible, cost-effective national and, where appropriate, regional programmes to improve the quality of local emission factors, activity data and/or models which reflect the socio-economic conditions of each Party for the preparation and periodic updating of national inventories of anthropogenic emissions by sources and removals by sinks of all greenhouse gases not controlled by the Montreal Protocol, using comparable methodologies to be agreed upon by the Conference of the Parties, and consistent with the guidelines for the preparation of national communications adopted by the Conference of the Parties;

(b) Formulate, implement, publish and regularly update national and, where appropriate, regional programmes containing measures to mitigate climate change and measures to facilitate adequate adaptation to climate change:

(i) Such programmes would, inter alia, concern the energy, transport and industry sectors as well as agriculture, forestry and waste management. Furthermore, adaptation technologies and methods for improving spatial planning would improve adaptation to climate change; and

(ii) Parties included in Annex I shall submit information on action under this Protocol, including national programmes, in accordance with Article 7; and other Parties shall seek to include in their national communications, as appropriate, information on programmes which contain measures that the Party believes contribute to addressing climate change and its adverse impacts, including the abatement of increases in greenhouse gas emissions, and enhancement of and removals by sinks, capacity building and adaptation measures;

(c) Cooperate in the promotion of effective modalities for the development, application and diffusion of, and take all practicable steps to promote, facilitate and finance, as appropriate, the transfer of, or access to, environmentally sound technologies, know-how, practices and processes pertinent to climate change, in particular to developing countries, including the formulation of policies and programmes for the effective transfer of environmentally sound technologies that are publicly owned or in the public domain and the creation of an enabling environment for the private sector, to promote and enhance the transfer of, and access to, environmentally sound technologies;

(d) Cooperate in scientific and technical research and promote the maintenance and the development of systematic observation systems and development of data archives to reduce uncertainties related to the climate system, the adverse impacts of climate change and the economic and social consequences of various response strategies, and promote the development and strengthening of endogenous capacities and capabilities to participate in international and intergovernmental efforts, programmes and networks on research and systematic observation, taking into account Article 5 of the Convention;

(e) Cooperate in and promote at the international level, and, where appropriate, using existing bodies, the development and implementation of education and training programmes, including the strengthening of national capacity building, in particular human and institutional capacities and the exchange or secondment of personnel to train experts in this field, in particular for developing countries, and facilitate at the national level public awareness of, and public access to information on, climate change. Suitable modalities should be developed to implement these activities through the relevant bodies of the Convention, taking into account Article 6 of the Convention;

(f) Include in their national communications information on programmes and activities undertaken pursuant to this Article in accordance with relevant decisions of the Conference of the Parties; and

(g) Give full consideration, in implementing the commitments under this Article, to Article 4, paragraph 8, of the Convention.

Article 11

1. In the implementation of Article 10, Parties shall take into account the provisions of Article 4, paragraphs 4, 5, 7, 8 and 9, of the Convention.

2. In the context of the implementation of Article 4, paragraph 1, of the Convention, in accordance with the provisions of Article 4, paragraph 3, and Article 11 of the Convention, and through the entity or entities entrusted with the operation of the financial mechanism of the Convention, the developed country Parties and other developed Parties included in Annex II to the Convention shall:

(a) Provide new and additional financial resources to meet the agreed full costs incurred by developing country Parties in advancing the implementation of existing commitments under Article 4, paragraph 1(a), of the

Convention that are covered in Article 10, subparagraph (a); and

(b) Also provide such financial resources, including for the transfer of technology, needed by the developing country Parties to meet the agreed full incremental costs of advancing the implementation of existing commitments under Article 4, paragraph 1, of the Convention that are covered by Article 10 and that are agreed between a developing country Party and the international entity or entities referred to in Article 11 of the Convention, in accordance with that Article.

The implementation of these existing commitments shall take into account the need for adequacy and predictability in the flow of funds and the importance of appropriate burden sharing among developed country Parties. The guidance to the entity or entities entrusted with the operation of the financial mechanism of the Convention in relevant decisions of the Conference of the Parties, including those agreed before the adoption of this Protocol, shall apply mutatis mutandis to the provisions of this paragraph.

Analysis: This paragraph requires developed countries such as Canada to pay for emissions reductions in the developing world. As with most United Nations spending plans, the United States was expected bear the largest burden, and although this section spoke generically about Annex II countries, it was understood that the U.S. would be the bankroller of this program. Since the unanimous U.S. Senate vote in 1997, rejecting Kyoto, these costs are now to be distributed among the remaining Annex II countries—including Canada.

Not only will Canada have to bear the expense of paying for its own emissions reductions—it will have to pay for them in Africa, Asia and Eastern Europe, too.

3. The developed country Parties and other developed Parties in Annex II to the Convention may also provide,

and developing country Parties avail themselves of, financial resources for the implementation of Article 10, through bilateral, regional and other multilateral channels.

Article 12

1. A clean development mechanism is hereby defined.

Analysis: Clean Development Mechanism is the name Kyoto gives to energy projects in the Third World that are sponsored by wealthy Kyoto countries. If a country cannot make its required greenhouse gas emissions reductions, that country can do a Kyoto-style repentance: It can spend money in a poor country, and buy itself forgiveness.

2. The purpose of the clean development mechanism shall be to assist Parties not included in Annex I in achieving sustainable development and in contributing to the ultimate objective of the Convention, and to assist Parties included in Annex I in achieving compliance with their quantified emission limitation and reduction commitments under Article 3.

3. Under the clean development mechanism:

(a) Parties not included in Annex I will benefit from project activities resulting in certified emission reductions; and

(b) Parties included in Annex I may use the certified emission reductions accruing from such project activities to contribute to compliance with part of their quantified emission limitation and reduction commitments under Article 3, as determined by the Conference of the Parties serving as the meeting of the Parties to this Protocol.

4. The clean development mechanism shall be subject to the authority and guidance of the Conference of the Parties serving as the meeting of the Parties to this Protocol and be supervised by an executive board of the clean development mechanism.

5. Emission reductions resulting from each project activity shall be certified by operational entities to be designated by the Conference of the Parties serving as the meeting of the Parties to this Protocol, on the basis of:

(a) Voluntary participation approved by each Party involved;

(b) Real, measurable, and long-term benefits related to the mitigation of climate change; and

(c) Reductions in emissions that are additional to any that would occur in the absence of the certified project activity.

6. The clean development mechanism shall assist in arranging funding of certified project activities as necessary.

7. The Conference of the Parties serving as the meeting of the Parties to this Protocol shall, at its first session, elaborate modalities and procedures with the objective of ensuring transparency, efficiency and accountability through independent auditing and verification of project activities.

8. The Conference of the Parties serving as the meeting of the Parties to this Protocol shall ensure that a share of the proceeds from certified project activities is used to cover administrative expenses as well as to assist developing country Parties that are particularly vulnerable to the adverse effects of climate change to meet the costs of adaptation.

9. Participation under the clean development mechanism, including in activities mentioned in paragraph 3(a) above and in the acquisition of certified emission reductions, may involve private and/or public entities, and is to be subject to whatever guidance may be provided by the executive board of the clean development mechanism.

10. Certified emission reductions obtained during the period from the year 2000 up to the beginning of the first commitment period can be used to assist in achieving compliance in the first commitment period.

Article 13

1. The Conference of the Parties, the supreme body of the Convention, shall serve as the meeting of the Parties to this Protocol.

2. Parties to the Convention that are not Parties to this Protocol may participate as observers in the proceedings of any session of the Conference of the Parties serving as the meeting of the Parties to this Protocol. When the Conference of the Parties serves as the meeting of the Parties to this Protocol, decisions under this Protocol shall be taken only by those that are Parties to this Protocol.

3. When the Conference of the Parties serves as the meeting of the Parties to this Protocol, any member of the Bureau of the Conference of the Parties representing a Party to the Convention but, at that time, not a Party to this Protocol, shall be replaced by an additional member to be elected by and from amongst the Parties to this Protocol.

4. The Conference of the Parties serving as the meeting of the Parties to this Protocol shall keep under regular review the implementation of this Protocol and shall make, within its mandate, the decisions necessary to promote its effective implementation. It shall perform the functions assigned to it by this Protocol and shall:

(a) Assess, on the basis of all information made available to it in accordance with the provisions of this Protocol, the implementation of this Protocol by the Parties, the overall effects of the measures taken pursuant to this Protocol, in particular environmental, economic and social effects as well as their cumulative impacts and the extent to which progress towards the objective of the Convention is being achieved;

(b) Periodically examine the obligations of the Parties under this Protocol, giving due consideration to any reviews required by Article 4, paragraph 2(d), and Article 7, paragraph 2, of the Convention, in the light of the objective of the Convention, the experience gained in its implementation and the evolution of scientific and technological knowledge, and in this respect consider and adopt regular reports on the implementation of this Protocol;

(c) Promote and facilitate the exchange of information on measures adopted by the Parties to address climate change and its effects, taking into account the differing circumstances, responsibilities and capabilities of the Parties and their respective commitments under this Protocol;

(d) Facilitate, at the request of two or more Parties, the coordination of measures adopted by them to address climate change and its effects, taking into account the differing circumstances, responsibilities and capabilities of the Parties and their respective commitments under this Protocol;

(e) Promote and guide, in accordance with the objective of the Convention and the provisions of this Protocol, and taking fully into account the relevant decisions by the Conference of the Parties, the development and periodic refinement of comparable methodologies for the effective implementation of this Protocol, to be agreed on by the Conference of the Parties serving as the meeting of the Parties to this Protocol;

(f) Make recommendations on any matters necessary for the implementation of this Protocol;

(g) Seek to mobilize additional financial resources in accordance with
Article 11, paragraph 2;

(h) Establish such subsidiary bodies as are deemed necessary for the implementation of this Protocol;

(i) Seek and utilize, where appropriate, the services and cooperation of, and information provided by, competent international organizations and intergovernmental and non-governmental bodies; and

(j) Exercise such other functions as may be required for

the implementation of this Protocol, and consider any assignment resulting from a decision by the Conference of the Parties.

5. The rules of procedure of the Conference of the Parties and financial procedures applied under the Convention shall be applied mutatis mutandis under this Protocol, except as may be otherwise decided by consensus by the Conference of the Parties serving as the meeting of the Parties to this Protocol.

6. The first session of the Conference of the Parties serving as the meeting of the Parties to this Protocol shall be convened by the secretariat in conjunction with the first session of the Conference of the Parties that is scheduled after the date of the entry into force of this Protocol. Subsequent ordinary sessions of the Conference of the Parties serving as the meeting of the Parties to this Protocol shall be held every year and in conjunction with ordinary sessions of the Conference of the Parties, unless otherwise decided by the Conference of the Parties serving as the meeting of the Parties to this Protocol.

7. Extraordinary sessions of the Conference of the Parties serving as the meeting of the Parties to this Protocol shall be held at such other times as may be deemed necessary by the Conference of the Parties serving as the meeting of the Parties to this Protocol, or at the written request of any Party, provided that, within six months of the request being communicated to the Parties by the secretariat, it is supported by at least one third of the Parties.

8. The United Nations, its specialized agencies and the International Atomic Energy Agency, as well as any State member thereof or observers thereto not party to the Convention, may be represented at sessions of the Conference of the Parties serving as the meeting of the Parties to this Protocol as observers. Any body or agency, whether national or international, governmental or non-governmental, which is qualified in matters covered by this Protocol and which has informed the secretariat of its

wish to be represented at a session of the Conference of the Parties serving as the meeting of the Parties to this Protocol as an observer, may be so admitted unless at least one third of the Parties present object. The admission and participation of observers shall be subject to the rules of procedure, as referred to in paragraph 5 above.

Article 14

1. The secretariat established by Article 8 of the Convention shall serve as the secretariat of this Protocol.

2. Article 8, paragraph 2, of the Convention on the functions of the secretariat, and

Article 8, paragraph 3, of the Convention on arrangements made for the functioning of the secretariat, shall apply mutatis mutandis to this Protocol. The secretariat shall, in addition, exercise the functions assigned to it under this Protocol.

Article 15

1. The Subsidiary Body for Scientific and Technological Advice and the Subsidiary Body for Implementation established by Articles 9 and 10 of the Convention shall serve as, respectively, the Subsidiary Body for Scientific and Technological Advice and the Subsidiary Body for Implementation of this Protocol. The provisions relating to the functioning of these two bodies under the Convention shall apply mutatis mutandis to this Protocol. Sessions of the meetings of the Subsidiary Body for Scientific and Technological Advice and the Subsidiary Body for Implementation of this Protocol shall be held in conjunction with the meetings of, respectively, the Subsidiary Body for Scientific and Technological Advice and the Subsidiary Body for Implementation of the Convention.

2. Parties to the Convention that are not Parties to this Protocol may participate as observers in the proceedings of any session of the subsidiary bodies. When the subsidiary bodies serve as the subsidiary bodies of this Protocol, decisions under this Protocol shall be

taken only by those that are Parties to this Protocol.

3. When the subsidiary bodies established by Articles 9 and 10 of the Convention exercise their functions with regard to matters concerning this Protocol, any member of the Bureaux of those subsidiary bodies representing a Party to the Convention but, at that time, not a party to this Protocol, shall be replaced by an additional member to be elected by and from amongst the Parties to this Protocol.

Article 16

The Conference of the Parties serving as the meeting of the Parties to this Protocol shall, as soon as practicable, consider the application to this Protocol of, and modify as appropriate, the multilateral consultative process referred to in Article 13 of the Convention, in the light of any relevant decisions that may be taken by the Conference of the Parties. Any multilateral consultative process that may be applied to this Protocol shall operate without prejudice to the procedures and mechanisms established in accordance with Article 18.

Article 17

The Conference of the Parties shall define the relevant principles, modalities, rules and guidelines, in particular for verification, reporting and accountability for emissions trading. The Parties included in Annex B may participate in emissions trading for the purposes of fulfilling their commitments under Article 3. Any such trading shall be supplemental to domestic actions for the purpose of meeting quantified emission limitation and reduction commitments under that Article.

Article 18

The Conference of the Parties serving as the meeting of the Parties to this Protocol shall, at its first session, approve appropriate and effective procedures and mechanisms to determine and to address cases of non-compliance with the provisions of this Protocol, including through the development of an indicative list of consequences, taking into account the cause, type, degree and frequency of non-compliance. Any procedures and mechanisms under this Article entailing binding consequences shall be adopted by means of an amendment to this Protocol.

Analysis: This is the punishment section of Kyoto. Countries that do not meet their emissions reduction targets will be subject to "a list of consequences." This section was written to give Kyoto teeth that Rio didn't have. Still, these consequences have not yet been written—that list of punishments requires an amendment to Kyoto.

Kyoto is a lose-lose proposition, from an economic point of view, for developed countries such as Canada. If Canada is to comply, we not only have to gut our own economy, but we are required to prop up inefficient, polluting economies in the developing world—including Russia. If we don't comply, this section threatens economic punishment, too.

Article 19
The provisions of Article 14 of the Convention on settlement of disputes shall apply mutatis mutandis to this Protocol.

Article 20
1. Any Party may propose amendments to this Protocol.
2. Amendments to this Protocol shall be adopted at an ordinary session of the Conference of the Parties serving as the meeting of the Parties to this Protocol. The text of any proposed amendment to this Protocol shall be communicated to the Parties by the secretariat at least six months before the meeting at which it is proposed for adoption. The secretariat shall also communicate the text of any proposed amendments to the Parties and signatories to the Convention and, for information, to the Depositary.
3. The Parties shall make every effort to reach agreement on any proposed amendment to this Protocol by consensus. If all efforts at consensus have been exhausted, and no agreement reached, the amendment shall as a last

resort be adopted by a three-fourths majority vote of the Parties present and voting at the meeting. The adopted amendment shall be communicated by the secretariat to the Depositary, who shall circulate it to all Parties for their acceptance.

4. Instruments of acceptance in respect of an amendment shall be deposited with the Depositary. An amendment adopted in accordance with paragraph 3 above shall enter into force for those Parties having accepted it on the ninetieth day after the date of receipt by the Depositary of an instrument of acceptance by at least three fourths of the Parties to this Protocol.

5. The amendment shall enter into force for any other Party on the ninetieth day after the date on which that Party deposits with the Depositary its instrument of acceptance of the said amendment.

Article 21

1. Annexes to this Protocol shall form an integral part thereof and, unless otherwise expressly provided, a reference to this Protocol constitutes at the same time a reference to any annexes thereto. Any annexes adopted after the entry into force of this Protocol shall be restricted to lists, forms and any other material of a descriptive nature that is of a scientific, technical, procedural or administrative character.

2. Any Party may make proposals for an annex to this Protocol and may propose amendments to annexes to this Protocol.

3. Annexes to this Protocol and amendments to annexes to this Protocol shall be adopted at an ordinary session of the Conference of the Parties serving as the meeting of the Parties to this Protocol. The text of any proposed annex or amendment to an annex shall be communicated to the Parties by the secretariat at least six months before the meeting at which it is proposed for adoption. The secretariat shall also communicate the text of any proposed annex or amendment to an annex to the Parties and sig-

natories to the Convention and, for information, to the Depositary.

4. The Parties shall make every effort to reach agreement on any proposed annex or amendment to an annex by consensus. If all efforts at consensus have been exhausted, and no agreement reached, the annex or amendment to an annex shall as a last resort be adopted by a three-fourths majority vote of the Parties present and voting at the meeting. The adopted annex or amendment to an annex shall be communicated by the secretariat to the Depositary, who shall circulate it to all Parties for their acceptance.

5. An annex, or amendment to an annex other than Annex A or B, that has been adopted in accordance with paragraphs 3 and 4 above shall enter into force for all Parties to this Protocol six months after the date of the communication by the Depositary to such Parties of the adoption of the annex or adoption of the amendment to the annex, except for those Parties that have notified the Depositary, in writing, within that period of their non-acceptance of the annex or amendment to the annex. The annex or amendment to an annex shall enter into force for Parties which withdraw their notification of non-acceptance on the ninetieth day after the date on which withdrawal of such notification has been received by the Depositary.

6. If the adoption of an annex or an amendment to an annex involves an amendment to this Protocol, that annex or amendment to an annex shall not enter into force until such time as the amendment to this Protocol enters into force.

7. Amendments to Annexes A and B to this Protocol shall be adopted and enter into force in accordance with the procedure set out in Article 20, provided that any amendment to Annex B shall be adopted only with the written consent of the Party concerned.

Article 22

1. Each Party shall have one vote, except as provided for in paragraph 2 below.

2. Regional economic integration organizations, in matters within their competence, shall exercise their right to vote with a number of votes equal to the number of their member States that are Parties to this Protocol. Such an organization shall not exercise its right to vote if any of its member States exercises its right, and vice versa.

Article 23

The Secretary-General of the United Nations shall be the Depositary of this Protocol.

Article 24

1. This Protocol shall be open for signature and subject to ratification, acceptance or approval by States and regional economic integration organizations which are Parties to the Convention. It shall be open for signature at United Nations Headquarters in New York from 16 March 1998 to 15 March 1999. This Protocol shall be open for accession from the day after the date on which it is closed for signature. Instruments of ratification, acceptance, approval or accession shall be deposited with the Depositary.

2. Any regional economic integration organization which becomes a Party to this Protocol without any of its member States being a Party shall be bound by all the obligations under this Protocol. In the case of such organizations, one or more of whose member States is a Party to this Protocol, the organization and its member States shall decide on their respective responsibilities for the performance of their obligations under this Protocol. In such cases, the organization and the member States shall not be entitled to exercise rights under this Protocol concurrently.

3. In their instruments of ratification, acceptance, approval or accession, regional economic integration organizations shall declare the extent of their competence with respect to the matters governed by this Protocol. These organizations shall also inform the Depositary, who shall in turn inform the Parties, of any substantial modification in the extent of their competence.

Article 25

1. This Protocol shall enter into force on the ninetieth day after the date on which not less than 55 Parties to the Convention, incorporating Parties included in Annex I which accounted in total for at least 55 per cent of the total carbon dioxide emissions for 1990 of the Parties included in Annex I, have deposited their instruments of ratification, acceptance, approval or accession.

2. For the purposes of this Article, "the total carbon dioxide emissions for 1990 of the Parties included in Annex I" means the amount communicated on or before the date of adoption of this Protocol by the Parties included in Annex I in their first national communications submitted in accordance with Article 12 of the Convention.

3. For each State or regional economic integration organization that ratifies, accepts or approves this Protocol or accedes thereto after the conditions set out in paragraph 1 above for entry into force have been fulfilled, this Protocol shall enter into force on the ninetieth day following the date of deposit of its instrument of ratification, acceptance, approval or accession.

4. For the purposes of this Article, any instrument deposited by a regional economic integration organization shall not be counted as additional to those deposited by States members of the organization.

Article 26

No reservations may be made to this Protocol.

Article 27

1. At any time after three years from the date on which this Protocol has entered into force for a Party, that Party may withdraw from this Protocol by giving written notification to the Depositary.

2. Any such withdrawal shall take effect upon expiry of one year from the date of receipt by the Depositary of the notification of withdrawal, or on such later date as may be specified in the notification of withdrawal.

3. Any Party that withdraws from the Convention shall be considered as also having withdrawn from this Protocol.

Analysis: This is the clause that allows countries to bail out of Kyoto—with one year's notice to the UN Of course, in practice, any country could effectively cease to participate in the treaty at any time, as the United Nations does not have legal authority to enforce the treaty over a sovereign country.

Article 28
The original of this Protocol, of which the Arabic, Chinese, English, French, Russian and Spanish texts are equally authentic, shall be deposited with the Secretary-General of the United Nations.
DONE at Kyoto this eleventh day of December one thousand nine hundred and ninety-seven.
IN WITNESS WHEREOF the undersigned, being duly authorized to that effect, have affixed their signatures to this Protocol on the dates indicated.

Annex A
Greenhouse gases
Carbon dioxide (CO_2), Methane (CH_4) Nitrous oxide, (N_2O) Hydrofluorocarbons (HFCs), Perfluorocarbons (PFCs), Sulphur hexafluoride (SF_6)
Sectors/source categories
Energy, Fuel combustion, Energy industries Manufacturing industries and construction Transport
Other sectors
Other
Fugitive emissions from fuels Solid fuels,
Oil and natural gas, Other Industrial processes,
Mineral products Chemical industry Metal production
Other production
Production of halocarbons and sulphur hexafluoride, Consumption of halocarbons and sulphur hexafluoride

Other
Solvent and other product use, Agriculture
Enteric fermentation, Manure management, Rice culti-
vation, Agricultural soils, Prescribed burning of
savannas, Field burning of agricultural residues Other
Waste, Solid waste disposal on land, Wastewater han-
dling, Waste incineration, Other

Analysis: Annex A is the list of emissions that are regulated
by Kyoto. Carbon dioxide is by far the most commonplace—and
by far the most harmless. There has never been a case of human
illness or death caused by atmospheric carbon dioxide. How
could there be, given that humans naturally exhale it?

The next gas listed is methane, otherwise known as natural
gas. It is itself a carbon-based fuel, and a very efficient fuel in
terms of its low pollution emissions. Besides its industrial sources
and uses, methane is produced naturally.

Nitrous oxide is another name for laughing gas. In addition
to industry, it is used by dentists as an anaesthetic, as a propulsion
gas for whipped cream dispensers, and by some auto racers to
increase performance of their engines.

The sectors/source categories list those industries that Kyoto
targets for reduction. It is not surprising that energy industries are
high up on Kyoto's enemies list. But even higher than energy
industries are energy users—what Kyoto calls "fuel combustion."
Anyone who drives a car, heats a home or office or takes the occasional plane trip is Kyoto's public enemy number one—even
worse than industry itself. That makes sense, because it is in the
burning of fuel that carbon dioxide is released, and that burning
happens in your car, not in an oil company's pipeline.

Kyoto lists other sectors—transportation, for example. That
in itself is weighted against Canada, for, unlike many of Europe's
mini-states, Canada has the second-largest land mass in the
world. Our use of energy in transportation will naturally be
higher than in Europe.

The list of other industries targeted shows that literally every
province in Canada will come under Kyoto scrutiny. The chemical

industries in Ontario and Quebec; mines in Nova Scotia and Ontario; metal production in Ontario, Quebec, and in the prospective Inco megaplant in Newfoundland and Labrador; and agriculture, from Quebec's dairy cows to Saskatchewan wheat farmers' use of diesel fuel to run their tractors.

Annex B
Party Quantified emission limitation or reduction commitment (percentage of base year or period)
Australia 108; Austria 92; Belgium 92; Bulgaria* 92; Canada 94; Croatia* 95; Czech Republic* 92; Denmark 92; Estonia* 92; European Community 92; Finland 92; France 92; Germany 92; Greece 92; Hungary* 94; Iceland 110; Ireland 92; Italy 92; Japan 94; Latvia* 92; Liechtenstein 92; Lithuania* 92; Luxembourg 92; Monaco 92; Netherlands 92; New Zealand 100; Norway 101; Poland* 94; Portugal 92; Romania* 92; Russian Federation* 100; Slovakia* 92; Slovenia* 92; Spain 92; Sweden 92; Switzerland 92; Ukraine* 100; United Kingdom of Great Britain and Northern Ireland 92; United States of America 93; * Countries that are undergoing the process of transition to a market economy.

Analysis: Annex B lists the emissions levels for each country, based on a percentage of their emissions in 1990. Of course, only some countries must actually reach those targets—so-called Annex II developed countries.

The European Union countries, as mentioned in earlier sections of Kyoto, can pool their emissions reductions, so that if one EU country cuts its emissions more than necessary, that can offset another EU country that hasn't met its goal.

Notice the absence of China, India, Brazil, Mexico, Venezuela or any of the Persian Gulf oil-producing countries, such as Saudi Arabia. Many of those countries will indeed "sign" Kyoto, but they are not required to make any emissions reductions whatsoever.

And notice, too, that many of the countries that signed Kyoto with such fanfare back in 1997—including Japan, the host country itself, have since declared that they cannot or will not follow through.

Finally, the U.S.—whose diplomats were happy to sign the treaty—pulled the plug on the deal when their Senate voted unanimously to forbid their country to be bound by Kyoto, unless it were to apply to all countries equally, and would not hurt the U.S. economy.